Other Authors' Praise for Deep Change

"This is an important book at a critical time in the life of our society, providing crucial insights as it deals with the paradoxes of gaining the world but losing its soul."
—Richard Tarnas, *The Passion of the Western World*

"Susan Plummer's book is a profound work of discovery. It is scholarly yet lyrical. It combines existential passion with epistemological depth in order to elucidate new stages in the structure of the human 'journey'; here is where her originality and insight shine through. This book will be a huge consolation and encouragement to our search for light."
—John O'Donohue, *Anam Cara*

"Dr. Plummer's model for personal change may be one of the most important contributions toward growth-centered counseling since Abraham Maslow's work on peak experience. The practical applications she describes make it easy to apply her principles, both for individuals guiding their own personal change and for professionals guiding others through theirs. I believe that this work will be a source of great personal breakthroughs for anyone committed to a path of personal and spiritual development."
—Hal Zina Bennett, Ph.D., *Lens of Perception*

What Readers Are Saying

"The first chapter described exactly what I had been going through! I had felt so lost and now I know that I am not alone and that there is a known way to move through it."
—28 Year Old Entertainment Industry Professional

"This book is so very invitational. I could just walk right into it and find myself. I recommend it highly to anyone going through periods of deep change, when life can appear so meaningless and without purpose."
—College Educator

"Through this larger framework and life vision, I find it easier to encourage my clients to trust and accept where they are, even through the bleakest times."
—Psychologist

"This is a model of real transformation. The applications are abundant and stunning!"
—Transpersonal Therapist And Author

"So good to have a map and a language for these strange yet vital human experiences! This book was a life-saver for me when I felt my life was literally going down the drain."
—Engineer

For Lois,

A kindred soul!
Looking forward to
future connections - all
the best with your
important and timely books!

Deep Change

Deep Change

Befriending the Unknown

Susan P. Plummer, Ph.D.

Tenacity Press

Published by
Tenacity Press
1-800-738-6721
www.TenacityPress.Org
Or at:
www.HalZinaBennett.com/tenacity_press.htm

Contact the author directly for
further information or permissions:
Plummer.DeepChange.Susan@GMail.com

Readers are cautioned that this book is not intended to replace advice or treatment for any health condition whatsoever.

To my son Ben,
for the pure joy of being his mother.
And in memory of Frances Crary
for her wise eldering.
And to John O'Donohue for his timely
and robust encouragement

Contents

Introduction

Do you sometimes have the feeling that your life has become meaningless? Do you find yourself wondering: "Is this it? Is this is all there is to life?" Do you experience a kind of inner emptiness that plagues you from time to time, or perhaps very often? Is there a growing sense that at its core, something is missing in your life? These feelings may have appeared as though out of the blue, or they may have arisen within a life crisis, such as a major loss, illness or other life change.

Whether these feelings are now in the foreground of your daily experience, or they are just beginning to nag at the periphery of your awareness, I want you to know the surprising good news that these feelings are the very signs that something new and wondrous has started in you. A new possibility for you, a new way of being in the world is calling you, one that is your birthright and will fulfill your deeper longings for greater connection, meaning and belonging.

Right now, the difficult and confusing feelings you are experiencing that are sometimes even hard to put into words, are the very evidence that you are being beckoned into a new depth, a new dimension we could say, one that will deliver you into the fullness you desire but cannot yet necessarily imagine. You are being called by something larger, something other than you that is longing for you even as you are longing for its promise of deeper fulfillment. If any of these statements ring true for you, welcome to the bewildering, challenging, enlivening and treasure-filled adventure I call "Deep Change!" And I want you to know that you are most definitely not alone in this journey. Many people are currently experiencing a loss of meaning, purpose and real connection in their lives. While these challenging times do indeed herald hidden promises, we at first understand only that something is very wrong with our lives. Something is amiss. We may feel flawed in a fundamental way. We may feel depressed, feel that we have little to contribute, that others have little or no place in our lives and that we have little or no place in theirs.

At these times, many people report that their lives are literally going down the drain. They want to feel better. They may reach out, sensing that there must be a way out of this place of meaninglessness and purposelessness. If there is, they certainly don't understand either the place where they presently stand or how to move beyond it. They may feel lost, helpless, perhaps anxious and afraid, seeking the faith, the tools and the direction to stay the full course until they arrive at a better place.

Whether you are on the threshold of the journey of Deep Change, or are in the midst of it, this book somehow got your attention or the attention of someone close to you who brought your attention to the book. As many of us are drawn into the journey of Deep Change (and there are indeed many of us), we encounter what I am describing as "the hole in your ocean" when every part of our being cries out that this is all wrong. How could it be that our lives have come to this!

At such times, it is easy to feel that there is no bottom to this emptiness, that this experience could not possibly have a good outcome. How could something that appears to be just the opposite of what we consciously want for our lives possibly bring us to a better place? We'll be exploring exactly that question in this book and why it is that by moving into our own fears and discomfort we can find the path to the greater depth, meaning and purpose that we are seeking.

Imagine for a moment that you are out on the ocean in a rowboat. Suddenly you realize you are further out than feels comfortable. Something feels awry, you are not sure what. You start to row back towards shore. But you feel the tug of a current carrying you further out to sea, away from the familiar and solid ground where you would feel secure. You feel your safety is threatened. Maybe you even feel panicked. You row hard, but it is of no use. The current is far stronger than you are. Now you hear a low rumble, like the tumbling water of a waterfall. As you are drawn closer, you see that it is a hole!

The water is being pulled down into a spiral vortex. It is being pulled down to...where? At this point, there is no way of knowing where this vortex is leading. This is the question before us whenever we are drawn into Deep Change. We will not know the answer to that question until we surrender to the power of the vortex and allow it to carry us to where we know not. This dynamic of letting go into the not-knowing is both the challenge and the promise of Deep Change.

When this first happened to me, in my late 20s, I recall having a mental image of a vast ocean with a hole in it, and the whole thing—my life—was draining out. What was worse, I had no idea how to stop it, to rescue myself, or to bring a sense of meaning and purpose back into my life. I saw no way to stop up the hole, no way to stop my ocean from emptying. The following description is an account of that time:

> *I began to experience a pervasive sense of meaninglessness. I had completed graduate school and was working for non-profit organizations doing meaningful and stimulating community projects. I lived in a beautiful rural area, owned my own home and had a good circle of friends. Yet everything seemed pointless. The world grew flat and empty and an oppressive stillness shrouded me, isolating me from any source that nurtured a meaningful*

relationship to the world and myself. There was no apparent cause or stimulus for my state, no recent loss, failure or crisis. On the contrary, everything in my life had the appearance of going along very well. Yet meaninglessness had entirely saturated my experience of my life, my world, and my self and there was no way out of it whatsoever.

Fortunately, I was seeing a gifted therapist who was both experienced and unusually wise in these matters. One day, while I was despairing over my absolute and unalterable sense of meaninglessness, she made a surprising and deceptively simple suggestion: "You're in meaninglessness now, Susan. So check it out, look around. What is it like? What do you notice?"

This was a startling idea for me! I had been so busy despairing over my state and trying to look for a way out, or at least a reason for my experience, it had never occurred to me that what I was calling meaninglessness could be an inhabitable territory worthy of exploration. My therapist had aroused in me a fragile flush of curiosity.

The next day, I came home from work feeling weary from the weeks of dread and meaninglessness. It was late afternoon in the middle of summer and my little home, flanked by two protective redwood trees, was invitingly cool and dark. I dropped my things, lay down on the couch and found myself thinking, "Okay, so now I'm in meaninglessness. What's it like being here?" It was then that I noticed that I could not imagine existing in the next moment. It wasn't that I wished to die, but I certainly felt that if there was a next moment, it wasn't there in any way I could perceive.

I could hardly breathe; after all, one needs a next moment to breathe into. But breathe I did, and the moment I took my next breath it was as if I had taken a step into nothingness. I recall the feeling even to this day, stepping forward with no assurance that there was any ground to hold me. But then I found myself getting up to take a walk. I didn't decide to take a walk, I just moved without any forethought. I stepped out on the porch in the summer dusk, and in that step I suddenly found myself in a different world. It was the same world as before, yet I was experiencing it in a totally different way.

Everything was shimmering and intensified. Colors and sounds and fragrances had new dimensions, an abundant contrast to the flat and bleak world of a moment ago, a mere breath ago. I was inside this new depth, held by it, belonging intimately to it.

Across the street a man was watering his yard. The stream of water coming from the hose was resounding as though coming from inside my ears, refreshing as it spilled through and over me while I walked through the twilight streets, the sights and sounds of children playing, the muffled tones of people on their porches sharing the day's end, the smell of fresh cut lawns and watered gardens, the subtle sweetness of jasmine and honeysuckle.

I was held by it all, by a gentle and warm substance that infused the world, a world in which I belonged without question, without the need to question. I was no longer seeking meaning nor was I feeling its absence. Meaning simply was everywhere and I was inside it. I didn't have to find or create it. It was larger than me, holding me.

What happened to me on that summer's eve? There was a mystery here. It was the first time I had come through the meaninglessness, apparently reaching some other side. I also knew that this progress had something to do with the fact that I had, for a time, fully accepted the meaninglessness I was experiencing. Since then, I have been most curious about the relationship between our experiences of meaninglessness and emptiness, and the arrival of a new and richer sense of connection, belonging and meaning, and this curiosity has guided my personal explorations as well as my academic research.

Many years have passed since that period of my life and what I've seen is that the secret of regaining the passion and meaning of my life wasn't at all in stopping up the hole. On the contrary, it had to do with looking more carefully at the vortex through which my ocean was emptying, for my life was not disappearing so much as being drawn into a new dimension of belonging, meaning and purpose.

In this book we will see that the truth of how we get to the fulfillment of our deepest longings is by stepping right into the very places we feel most vulnerable. This truth is not common knowledge. Most of us are, instead, taught since infancy to turn away from the places of greatest vulnerability within ourselves. We are encouraged to try to rise above, fix and ignore the threshold experiences of Deep Change such as meaninglessness, a sense of lack, a sense of being flawed or inadequate.

In our world today, there are seemingly infinite numbers of remedies and palliatives promising to interrupt, or even stop forever, the process I'm describing here. These can range from getting a prescription for the newest psychotropic drug, to imbibing intoxicants, to going on a long vacation, or acquiring something new such as a car or home or even a different spouse. Any of these can dull the pain and discomfort we are feeling, or at least take our minds off what we're feeling. Some can literally change our brain chemistry so that whatever we're experiencing ceases to matter to us.

What this means, however, is that you may be blocking important signals for change that your entire being is sending to you. It is impossible to estimate the cost to us in terms of delayed or aborted personal development, or what impact these ill-advised palliatives might have on our society.

If we fully understood the dynamics of Deep Change, we would be more likely to welcome these challenging feelings and times in our lives. I want to propose to you a vision of what our experience might be like if we were to live in a community that embraced and recognized the significance of Deep Change. This vision illustrates how far we, as a culture, currently are from what I believe is needed.

What if you lived in a world where, when you began to feel lost and empty, your life flooded with a sense of meaninglessness, there were wise elders keeping their eyes out for you, watching you, and they celebrated the appearance of these experiences in you, because it meant that you were being called into new growth, into a new way of being, a coming of age, so to speak, a next phase of maturation. And how would you feel if this next phase was widely understood by those around you, not as pushing you toward your ability to be on your own, competent and independent, but as your evolving ability to join more intimately with the world, to be radically receptive, to be more collaborative, to co-create with new dimensions, and to connect and belong more deeply and authentically with your self and your world.

What would that be like, to be so honored, protected and celebrated because those around you understood that these challenging experiences are signs that you are entering a valuable new phase of development? And what if you knew at the outset that forces around you would gather to help you through this journey? There would be a circle of those elders experienced in the territory of Deep Change who would offer you a conceptual understanding to give you faith that this is where you need to go. They would mentor you and offer you tools to support your journey so that you could open safely to the riches that await you! What would it be like to live in that kind of world?

I may have the privilege of being the first person to welcome you into the journey of Deep Change and to congratulate you because these difficult and confusing feelings that you are not able or willing to put aside, mean that the tug in you to grow and become more of who you truly are has become stronger than your desire to stay on familiar ground, and that a deeper dimension in the world is exerting its longing for you. I wish to go a lot further than welcoming you. I wish to provide you with a kind of map to help you negotiate the experience of Deep Change. And I wish to offer you the understanding and tools that I know will prove to be useful guides and footholds.

In writing this book I have hoped to outline the particular challenges and promises of Deep Change so that you and others might have a broader perspective about the nature of such change, its promise, and what's actually involved when you choose to move through it. I believe that the hope for our future, both personal and societal, may well be found in our ability to cooperate with and safely navigate these forces of Deep Change, rather than sidestepping them.

We are all facing a critical juncture in our individual lives as well as in our culture as a whole. You may feel alienated from the world as the forces of Deep Change take hold of your life, but again, please know that you are most definitely not alone. Many people are feeling the pull of the hole in their respective oceans. Each of us will experience this process in our own way, with varying details, duration and intensity.

Seven Shifts of Deep Change

There are seven major common experiential shifts that we move through in Deep Change, regardless of our individual life circumstances. These are: 1) The Unsettling; 2) The Opening; 3) The Unraveling; 4) The Stilling; 5) The Releasing; 6) The Spreading, and 7) The Holding. These seven shifts of Deep Change, and how they relate to one another, grow out of my own investigation, designed to reveal what we are experience-ing as we are living through this phenomenon. This means that the material in this book is describing an organic human experience, as opposed to imposing some kind of theory or model onto our experience. The seven shifts describe what we experience naturally, when we allow ourselves to open to the journey of Deep Change.

Another essential aspect of the material in this book is that it brings the entire experience of Deep Change, *as a whole*, into focus. In other words, it not only describes each individual shift but also shows us how the shifts move into and away from one another. I believe you will find this understanding of the whole dynamic of Deep Change to be both fruitful and reassuring.

Notes on Reading This Book

As you read, it will be helpful to realize that each of the seven shifts describes a progressive degree of letting go of our familiar way of being in the world, allowing ourselves to open up to a different, unfamiliar way of being. Each shift has different characteristics, challenges and promises, and each asks of us a certain kind of cooperation and support. There are many variations as to how and when people experience these seven shifts, such as different life contexts and different degrees of intensity. Also, individuals can go through the cycle of Deep Change many times in their lives and again, to varying degrees.

But keep in mind that the seven shifts provide guidelines for you. You might recognize certain shifts and not others. Also, it is important to know that a person does not necessarily march through these shifts in some very neat and orderly progression. One person might be dwelling in one shift for a very long time, or another person may move through the same shift in a blink of an eye. I encourage you to not be concerned about "doing this right." Rather, use the material more as a map, one that can help you to orient yourself.

As you find yourself in the book's material, let yourself be supported by it. Let yourself be comforted, knowing that having a map means that others have gone this way before you, and that through their journey they discovered the fulfillment of their longings for deeper meaning, connection and belonging. As you read, step back every once in a while and reflect on how these shifts are working in concert with one another. They have a kind of rhythm, a movement where one flows out of and into another. This relationship is perhaps even more important than the individual characteristics of each shift.

To support your understanding of the overall movements of the shifts, I have included, in the appendix, several diagrams that illustrate the flow from one shift into another. You may find them useful. But if this is not the case, just pass over them. The hazard of such illustrations is that they appear, at least in a book, as static constructs. It is very important to keep in mind that the diagrams show the movement throughout the shifts, the movement of our experience and awareness. It may help to think of them as visual metaphors.

This material is breaking some new ground, and while I provide examples and anecdotes for each shift, I also have needed to describe and explain quite a few new ideas and to introduce new phrases. As you read along, don't worry if the ideas I present here are not all clear to you right away, but let yourself keep moving through the material. As you do this you will find that something will start moving in you, evolving a deeper trust in this journey, a dawning recognition of something very deep and natural in you that some part of you already knows.

Through this book my desire is that this organic and dynamic *human-becoming* will come into greater visibility so that we can see it and recognize it together and have a language to talk with one another about it. It is also my hope that this book will offer you a sense of companionship as you travel through Deep Change, so that you can feel the presence and wisdom of the fellow travelers who have journeyed along this path before. And finally, I invite you to be part of a continued exploration of the experience of Deep Change by sharing your story, your variations, struggles, and what has helped you along the way. I would be very happy to hear from you.

...what is healthy is usually at first unsettling. It becomes necessary not to immediately reject the disturbance but to go on to see whether a whole world is being revealed.
—Robert Sardello

Shift 1: The Unsettling

One of the great contradictions of human life is that we seek change even as we cling to the way things are. When these two impulses are relatively equal, we experience life as coherent and stable; there seem to be few if any disconcerting mysteries, and life's challenges are relatively easy to resolve. We might feel the undercurrent of tensions between the desire to change and the desire to keep things as they are but life generally appears to be quite manageable.

If the tension to change becomes more compelling than the tension to stay the same, however, it is often accompanied by feelings that something is missing from our life, which is best described as a *felt lack*. I use this term to describe the experience because, where Deep Change is involved, we are most often not immediately able to identify the exact nature of what's lacking. We only sense and feel a lack. In the absence of there being any way to explain the felt lack in terms of our familiar self-and-world, our primary experience is one of a *free-*

floating longing, a yearning for something we cannot yet identify.

A pressure building within us now seems to be drawing us out of the familiar into the unknown and into the desire for change. We might be experiencing a strange mixture of feelings at this time—no longer satisfied with the way things are, maybe lacking confidence in our own knowledge or skills, and perhaps seeking answers to questions that we struggle to articulate.

Doubts and anxieties grow as confidence in our familiar way of being begins to slip away from us. Activities and relationships we once enjoyed, sources of pleasure that once brought us deep personal satisfaction, no longer grace our lives. As this pattern continues, the feeling that life has no meaning or purpose intensifies. Nagging questions about meaning and purpose move into the foreground of our awareness. Whereas we might have once been able to deny these nagging feelings, or push them into the background, we no longer can. Something seems to be calling from the outside as well as from within us. Deep down inside we begin to suspect that there is no turning back to the familiar world where we once found relative comfort.

As the pleasures and satisfactions of our familiar world fade away we enter what I call the "Unsettling," the first shift that will draw us increasingly toward Deep Change. The Unsettling can move in on us gradually and subtly, yet also unrelentingly, so that we may feel as if the whole world is closing in around us. Just as often, we can awaken one morning and, seemingly with no prior warning, feel as if our entire world has lost its depth. We may find ourselves wondering, "Has my life always been this flat and shallow and colorless?"

One woman, Janice, tells how on her way to her teaching job at the university one morning she had to pull over to the side of the road. "It came upon me so suddenly," she said. "At first I was terrified. I wasn't in real pain like doctors describe when you have a heart attack, so I knew it wasn't something like that. But I sure felt heavy of heart, just leaden...and disconnected. I felt like if I sat there at the side of the road for the rest of my life, with the cars and trucks whizzing past me, it wouldn't have mattered to me or anyone else at all. What was the point? If you'd asked me the day before if I liked teaching, I'm sure I would have told you I loved it, and would have meant it, as far as I could tell. Even the things I'd once loved to do now seemed pointless and barren, nothing but a big vacuum—and I had been sucked right into it. My whole life was phony and, most important, so was I. Not that even *that* mattered....because it didn't. Nothing did."

As the Unsettling deepens, you may begin to experience yourself as *unreal,* moving into a way of being that is strange and difficult to grasp. And yet, you may continue to operate in the world pretty much as you did before. You go to work, do what needs to be done, come home and plod through the routine of your family life, yet you feel as if you have taken on an alien identity and seemingly your life has nothing to do with who you are. Your self-identity is up for question. *Who am I? What am I doing here? What is anyone doing here?*

What has happened to my sense of belonging? As you start asking questions such as these, no answers come back. You come up empty, disconnected, and life as you've known it feels out of control.

As your experience of the Unsettling progresses, you may find it difficult to get out of bed in the morning. You might feel lethargic and weary, uninterested in anything. You might, for a while, pump yourself up, working up the energy to care, to move forward, but these efforts are hollow at best, becoming increasingly impossible to initiate.

Having tried everything you know to make yourself feel better, your sense of helplessness increases and you may begin to panic. And as if things weren't bad enough, the people around you don't want to hear you tell about what you're experiencing. At worst, they avoid you. At best, they make suggestions, diagnosing your *illness* or trying to *fix* you. Friends offer you the names of therapists or tell you about pharmaceuticals which have helped them get over similar discomforts. One person reported: "My best friend just tells me to get over it. She tells me that when she feels like that, she goes shopping." While this may sound flippant, even humorous, it's important to recognize that the symptoms of the Unsettling can be threatening for other people to hear about. The feelings of being without meaning and purpose border on sacrilege in our Western World, where our value to others often centers on being positive, independent, productive, and self-actualizing. For the moment, you are feeling anything but!

While the picture I paint here clearly characterizes the Unsettling, you are not necessarily feeling all of these things at once, or you might be experiencing them to a greater or lesser degree than I describe. In addition, many people learn to adapt to these feelings by developing behaviors to get themselves through. They may continue to go about their everyday lives in a way that seems normal to the people around them. Maybe they appear a bit more moody than usual. Maybe they are a bit distant. Maybe they even seem apathetic or depressed at times. But these behaviors are often passed over as temporary. The explanation that "everyone goes through periods like that," is an effort to explain away something that isn't at all that simple.

If you are reading this book the chances are quite good that you or a loved one are in the midst of the Unsettling. Perhaps you're uncomfortable or even seriously worried or distressed about your friend's or your own behavior. Any of the efforts that usually work to reduce or move beyond the symptoms either are not working or are not working well. As a result, you are seeking a way to more constructively address the issues and get back to *the way things were*—or at least to a more comfortable place.

To maintain some perspective during this difficult time, you might remind yourself that the source of your discomfort comes from the fact that your familiar self, as well as your familiar world, has already begun moving toward change. Where only a short time ago your old ways of making sense of your life gave your life meaning and purpose, they now feel incomplete or maybe no longer even apply. One person described the feeling of this shift as *being in a limbo state.* While you may experience the free-floating yearning that will eventually guide you toward feeling complete again, you have no idea how to proceed. If you can fully grasp the role of the Unsettling in your life—and be assured that there is a way through it—some of the panic you might be feeling will be reduced, freeing your energy for the work that Deep Change demands.

Good News About The Unsettling

As uncomfortable as the Unsettling experience might be, it is good news, providing that you are willing to set aside preconceived ideas about it and develop the courage required to be present with what you're feeling. The kind of courage required is not the heroic roll-up-your-sleeves-and-get-to-work kind but is heroic never the less. It will require a commitment and a lot of heart and patience. What's required is your willingness to acknowledge that you *do not know the answers,* and that you do not, at this point, need to be in charge of the outcome. The fact is, because of the nature of Deep Change itself, you cannot be in charge of the outcome since you cannot know the future toward which you are moving.

Not knowing is the key here, much more than *knowing.* Rather than attempting to take charge of the outcome, you will be learning how to become more attentive, in a vulnerable, accepting way, to what presently feels confusing, alien or even forbidding to you.

Like everything else in the Unsettling, what will get you through can often seem like just the opposite. You try to take command of your life, to control what's troubling you, when the only way to find the path ahead is to let go, to have a willingness to be attentive and vulnerable to what's happening right now within you...moment to moment to moment.

It can be helpful to approach this time of the Unsettling as a mystery. What's sometimes difficult to grasp is that the yearning we feel comes from an inner drive to move beyond our habitual ways of being, moving us beyond our present knowing into a new relationship with ourselves and the world.

Ted, who was a civil engineer, at first described his experience of the Unsettling as "hitting the wall." At 43, he had his own thriving business, was married and had two children in middle school. The Unsettling came upon him soon after signing one of the largest contracts of his life. He was happy about getting the business but soon after the first planning sessions with his staff, he said, "It was like the bottom dropped out of my world." Ordinarily, these initial planning meetings excited him. It was a time when he put together the big picture of what had to be done, thus mapping out work schedules and assigning any subcontracts that might be involved. That day, however, he turned the meeting over to his assistant and left. He explained, "I just got into my car and drove, never even thinking about where I was going or why. An hour later I kind of came to and discovered I was in Centerville, fifty miles from home."

Ted made an appointment with his doctor the next day and for two weeks was subjected to nearly every medical test in the world. Nothing, however, was found except that he had slightly elevated blood pressure. In the ensuing months, he did what he'd always done when he was feeling down or at loose ends: he went out looking for new projects. He had always loved signing on new projects, explaining that it made him feel he was "in control of my life." This time around, nothing he tried seemed to work. In fact, he noted, everything he tried "only seemed to deepen my sense of my life being empty and pointless."

Ted had never considered seeking personal help from a psychologist or other personal counselor, so when he came to me he was both nervous and skeptical. His dubiousness faded, however, when he saw how closely his experiences and symptoms matched those of other Deep Change clients. While it was difficult for him to believe that his efforts to take greater control of his life were only intensifying the Unsettling, he eventually accepted this concept and soon moved beyond this first shift. As he worked through the shifts, he came to some deeply personal realizations that allowed him to turn to what he described as "more creative endeavors" in his business, something he'd been wanting to do for several years.

Ted's case illustrates how, if you are willing to embrace the mystery of the Unsettling and enter this territory with an open spirit of discovery, you will, as Thoreau says, "meet with success unexpected." In a very real way, the Unsettling is the start of a journey into the realization of your true human birthright, into discovering your true identity, beyond what you presently might even be able to imagine. From the perspective of the free-floating longing of this period of the Unsettling, you're having the earliest awareness of there being a new way of relating to the world, one that is beyond the familiar self-and-world identity you now hold.

Above all else, the Unsettling indicates that your yearning for change and growth has moved into a dominant position above your desire to stay the same. While you may still feel resistance to change, you are drawing away from that resistance; as you do this you may feel some increased tension. The more you come to accept that your discomfort indicates positive movement —this book is intended to help with that—the more you will appreciate what your confusion is all about, and the more your fears will diminish. You'll move away from feeling that "something has gone seriously wrong" and develop the perspective that you are safely crossing into a new way of being, following a path that will bring you into living your life more fully and more deeply.

Accepting the Unacceptable

As you contemplate what's going on with you, only one thing seems certain: living in the Unsettling is uncomfortable. It's certainly not the way you're accustomed to feeling, and the longer it goes on the more difficult it is to convince yourself that things are going to turn out okay.

There's a part of us that will indeed insist that something's wrong. It's the same part that alerts you to take action when you are sick or injured. It's the part that tells you to take your hand out of the fire before you get burned, or that tells you to be cautious when crossing busy streets. But for the time being, and in the specific shift that the Unsettling represents, you need to do something that may indeed seem to run counter to your self-protective instincts. Instead of trying to escape the discomfort, you will need to pay more attention to it, to become more fully present with it, as uncomfortable and counter-intuitive as that might seem to be.

If you follow this course, as Ted did, you'll discover that the Unsettling is leading you to another way of experiencing yourself in relation to the world. A new awareness is exerting a pull on you that is both powerful and disruptive. Life-as-usual is no longer enough for you.

How has this happened? What is pulling you into this unsettled and disruptive state of being? You might look outside yourself for an explanation but find nothing, and the more you search the worse things seem to get. That's because the Unsettling comes both from within you and from beyond you—manifesting primarily as a feeling that something is missing even as you may be feeling a beckoning from sources outside you. Some people may, with 20/20 hindsight, say that it started as the result of a particular epiphany, or following a crisis, or as the result of a personal breakthrough. However, this is not always the case. You may or may not be able to point to a particular event in your life and say, *this is it. It started here.*

To clarify why that is so, consider this: Each of us has our own unique way of making sense of the world, of giving order, meaning and a sense of purpose to our daily experiences. We weave patterns of meaning from the fibers of what we've felt, thought, observed and believed. This tapestry of woven meanings is our *self-and-world structure*. What is this structure? It is a complex of personal perceptions about our role in the world, as well as perceptions about how the world *should* work. We constantly measure our experiences against this structure, making choices according to what it tells us is meaningful or meaningless. Through our self-and-world-structure we make sense of our lives—but even as we are making sense of our world we limit what we are capable of experiencing. In a very real way, who we are is contained by this self-and-world structure, holding us within its tensions of interwoven threads, just as a weaving of wool and other fibers is held together by its many strands, determining a particular pattern.

Ted's case is interesting in that, early in his life he had quite deliberately defined his self-and-world-structure consistent with the engineering disciplines that had beckoned to him early in his youth. Those early choices not only helped him to build a very successful engineering company but it would also affect how he functioned in his family and private life. Everything he did was well thought out, rational and deliberate. Yet, as he met the challenge of the Unsettling and moved through the shifts of Deep Change, he opened into a deeper part of himself, one that was playful, insightful, and inventive. Eventually, he recognized that something outside him had beckoned to this more open, creative, and flexible part of himself, producing his Unsettling and the yearning that would finally motivate him to seek and change certain aspects of his life.

While our self-and-world-structure has its own integrity, it is also responsive to and affected by the world beyond us. What changes you, bringing you into this place of the Unsettling, often appears to come only from within you. The *felt lack* you experience at the outset triggers your questioning, causing you to seek whatever it might be to fill that felt lack, like seeking the missing piece of a jigsaw puzzle. What Ted and others ultimately found, however, was that the Unsettling is triggered not only from within us but from a source *other than us* and which is *outside us.* As one person put it, *"Something outside me, something out there in the world yearns for me as much as I yearn for it."*

Here's an image that might help explain this dual nature of the forces of change: Research has shown that during the early stages of birth, certain hormones are released by the baby while it is still in the womb, signaling the mother's body to start the birthing process. But I think there's more to it than that; it is my belief that the birthing process is energized by both the desire of the baby to come into the world and the desire of the world to have this new being come in.

The novelist Graham Greene spoke of the moment "when the door opens and lets the future in."[1] What we need to see in this process is that the future calls us to

---

[1] Greene, Graham. *The Power and The Glory*

open that door, and it is in this calling, and our response to it, that the energy of the Unsettling is kindled.

The awareness of something missing, perhaps awakened by recognizing the world's call, alerts us to a potential for living in a deeper and more expansive way. Our tendency, then, is to look within ourselves, searching for a lack that needs to be filled, or for something "wrong" that needs to be fixed. Search though we might, we cannot find within our present self-and-world structure anything that will satisfy our yearning. If we're to satisfy this yearning, we need to move beyond our current way of relating to life. We need to recognize and answer the call.

It's About You

Whether or not you can identify when or how it began, the Unsettling is all about you. The possibilities you've consciously or unconsciously glimpsed are real, though you may not yet be able to say what they are or bring them into focus enough to experience them. The reason you can't is that—at least for now—you are unable to manifest this new possibility from within your own familiar perceptions of who you are and what your world is about.

Meanwhile, you may find yourself unable to name your yearning, hovering instead in a place of unknowing. *Yearning for what?* Shouldn't you be able to describe and name what you're seeking? The answer is no, you can't yet name or describe it because it does not yet exist within the world you presently know. You know it is there only because you experience the felt lack. Whatever it is that creates this felt lack is literally outside yourself. The following verse from "Have You Ever," by the musical group *Off Spring*, offers an apt description of the felt lack and free-floating longing we experience in the Unsettling:

> *Have you ever felt like there was more—*
> *like someone else was keeping score*
> *and what could make you whole*
> *was simply out of reach?*

Why does your present life come up short at this point? It is because some part of you has moved ahead of your self, catching at least a glimpse of the fuller existence that is held in the promise of what calls you from the outside. Meanwhile, the felt lack which you are experiencing comes from the fact that you are still living through the perspectives of your old way of knowing and seeing the world. Whatever glimpse you might have had of the fuller existence clearly signals to you that you are missing something. This sense of missing something is called the "felt lack" because you *feel* it. It is not an abstract idea at all. It is a subjective but unmistakable *feeling*. Like the free-floating longing at the start of the Unsettling, it is difficult to get a handle on and even more difficult to ignore.

While the felt lack works in partnership with the *free-floating longing*, you may initially be aware only of the felt lack. However, it can be extremely important to be able to experience the longing as well. The longing draws you toward the unknown—which is the only place where you can hope to find what you are seeking.

The energy of your yearning—which we now understand as a combination of the outer calling and the inner sense of lack—exerts a force on your known self-and-world structure, ultimately creating an *opening* in that structure. This opening, Shift 2 of Deep Change, is covered in the next chapter. With the opening you find that your acceptance of what's happening to you in the Unsettling is leading you deeper into yourself, where you now catch glimpses of an expanding self making way for that which will answer your felt lack.

Sensing Your Free-Floating Longing

As you negotiate the journey of Deep Change it is helpful to become aware of your longing. This does not mean that you clearly identify the nature of this longing or even the felt lack toward which it points. Rather, what you want to get in touch with is the *sense of the pull* associated with the yearning, of something outside you yearning for connection. You will feel this in your body rather than intellectually understanding it.

Since the yearning is palpable, it can help you develop your faith that some new possibility really is out there exerting its pull in your life. Detecting the pull of your free-floating longing allows you to move beyond any despair or resignation you're experiencing and let go of any concepts of *lack* or *shortcoming* in yourself. Instead, as you allow yourself to be drawn ahead by the longing, you'll realize it's signaling new possibilities, not pointing back at a shortcoming.

As you ask yourself the following questions, write down your answers, record them on your computer, or tell them to a friend:

1. What are you experiencing that you are wanting to change? Describe your feelings. (Helps you focus in on your felt lack.)

2. What are you presently doing to try to feel better? (May show you how you are presently trying to fill your felt lack.)

3. Imagine how you might feel if you were able to make the changes in exactly the way you wish. Describe these feelings. (May begin to reveal your longing.)

As you become more aware of how you'd like to feel in your relationship with yourself and your world, sit quietly and gently see if you can feel a tug within you. This longing might feel like a heartache or nostalgia. Just let whatever you are feeling come to the forefront. The point is simply to allow the experience of yearning to be there, without trying to figure it out or determine what to do with it, or to try to make it go away. If you can only let yourself sense your longing for a few seconds, this is a significant step.

You might also experiment with letting your attention drift back to childhood, to a particular time when you experienced yourself as innocent and free. See if you can recall those early dreams for the world and for what your life would become. You might feel sadness as you get in touch with dreams that never came true for you. Or you might feel bad for other reasons. If this happens, allow yourself to grieve what is past. To do so is to release yourself from the past so that you can move forward.

While opening up to feelings of nostalgia or heartache that might be associated with your early dreams and hopes, allow yourself to open to new possibilities. This may seem painful at first, but what we frequently find is that getting in touch with the feelings of those early dreams connects us with the free-floating longing that is beckoning to us now, urging us toward Deep Change. It may be helpful right now to realize that your present opening to new possibilities is stirring up disappointments and hurts that have dulled your ability to yearn.

The awakening of your yearning for Deep Change is a priceless gift. As you awaken it within yourself, just let it be as it is. Let it live within you, feeling its pull without attempting to control or analyze where it might be leading you. This may not be easy since it can possibly involve letting in experiences of emptiness, sorrow, and grief.

Much of what our health professionals are labeling as *depression* has its origins in our efforts to cover over or dull ourselves to the Unsettling we are experiencing. Such depression can be so successful that it covers over any and all awareness of new possibilities. The energy you might expend trying to bury feelings of potential change can leave you exhausted and lethargic, operating as if on automatic pilot and with little or no interest in your life.

In the more common type of depression, we still have a sense of discontent and meaninglessness, with the Unsettling always hovering close at hand.

The experience of anxiety often indicates that you are indeed in the midst of the Unsettling. It may well be the way you first register the beginning awareness of a coming change.

In the pages ahead, we'll be looking at anxiety and depression in ways that are quite different from those of modern Western cultures. We'll examine them not as pathologies, or as experiences we need to block or rectify but within the larger context of Deep Change.

A Note on the Cultural Implications of Deep Change

Depression and anxiety have risen to epidemic proportions in our society. There is tremendous pressure to succeed, fueled by growing economic concerns and a breakdown of support systems such as family and community. All of these contribute to our anxiety and depression, but I would argue that our entire culture is poised on the brink of Deep Change. We are all Unsettled. Crises everywhere are pointing to the fact that we are not who we thought we were. A discussion about how our culture is in the midst of Deep Change is included in the conclusion of this book under "Deep Change of the Collective."

For now, please recognize that when we are experiencing the shifts of Deep Change in our individual lives while in the midst of widespread cultural changes, it can be exceptionally easy to feel that each one of us is alone. Take heart if this is the case for you. Even though you might feel that you are alone and adrift, rest assured that there are a great many others like yourself out there, individuals who are experiencing a profound sense of Unsettling. The intent of this book is to help you, and millions like you the world over, to feel less isolated and to recognize and trust your Unsettling. It is time for us all to recognize and trust the Unsettling for what it really is—a process for developing new ways to cooperate with life's desire to bring us into a deeper experience of personal freedom, meaning, connection, security and belonging.

Ring the bells that still can ring
Forget your perfect offering
There is a crack in everything
That's what lets the light in
—Leonard Cohen

Shift 2: The Opening

In Shift 1, the Unsettling, we encountered the feeling that our lives were off kilter and we could no longer cover up this feeling that something was either missing or fundamentally wrong. We perhaps searched for ways to correct something within us, but to no avail.

We now move into Shift 2 where we find that the only thing we can ultimately do is to accept that we are helpless to change what we are feeling. We are not resigning ourselves to the feelings of Shift 1, nor are we giving in to despair, though at first it may seem that way. Rather, in our acceptance of our helplessness we are getting out of our own way and allowing our self and our world to be just as they are. Once we do this and begin to move into Shift 2, we discover that what we had experienced as a lack, a flaw, or an emptiness, now leads us into new depths and richness within ourselves. One person described it this way:

I was feeling a vague emptiness behind me, always there, following me everywhere. No matter what I did, it was there, making me feel somewhat unreal, keeping me from feeling really part of the world. The more I tried to do things to make this shadow of emptiness go away, the worse it became. Then one day, exhausted and defeated–without energy or the desire to try to move away from or fill the emptiness, I turned around, so to speak, and faced this nagging, persistent presence. I looked at it openly to see what it was and as I just looked–and as soon as I looked– I no longer was moving away from what I had been feeling so much as I was moving into it, actually merging with the sense of emptiness.

At any rate, it was now inside of me. And as I just felt this emptiness I seemed to move into another part of me. I'd say it was like moving into parts of me I hadn't known about before, deeper into who I am. I joined with a very real sense of me–I just felt completely me, totally with what I was feeling and experiencing. I was surrounded in an experience of deep sadness but also a welcoming...all of it wrapped up together.

This is the great secret of Shift 2 that we'll be exploring in this chapter: Through the kind of acceptance that allowed the above writer to move into the experiences of emptiness, you can move from trying to *do* something about your felt lack to *embracing* what you have been experiencing. Shift 2 is about dwelling within those feelings and experiences instead of attempting to manage, explain, control or otherwise get them to go away. Through the teachings of Shift 2 you come into a place in your life where you can allow the experience of yearning or lack to be just as it is. Having given up trying to change what you're feeling, you soon discover that all efforts to extricate yourself, or numb these feelings, have only kept you from moving on. Put another way, you discover that your efforts to solve the problem *is the problem.*

Your movement towards acceptance in Shift 2 can occur in the wink of an eye or can involve a long struggle. Make no judgment about the duration, for the time you spend in Shift 2 is dependent on many, highly individualized factors that are impossible to anticipate at the beginning of your journey. It is possible to stand in your own way and prolong the process unnecessarily but by seeing what is involved, which you will be doing in this chapter, you can allow the process to unfold in a way that is cohesive and effective.

If it helps, think of yourself being drawn along by a mysterious creative current, one that is pulling *for* you, not *against* you. Think of this current as drawing you into a greater, richer depth of yourself rather than diminishing you. Whereas in Shift 1 you encountered the free-floating longing and sense of lack, and could not find a way to ease that longing or fill that sense of lack, in Shift 2 you learn a way of being that can allow this disruption of your world, revealing an opening into your own greater depths of being.

Acceptance and Helplessness

The biggest hazard in this shift is misunderstanding what it means to *accept your helplessness.* During this shift, it can be easy to think of acceptance as giving in to the problem, of sinking into fatalistic acquiescence. This is not the case. What Shift 2 reveals is that acceptance dynamically clears away the obstacles to change. You may feel absolutely stuck, helpless, full of anxiety and dread, but even as you are feeling these things, there is a deeper truth to remember, which we explored in Shift 1: these feelings mean you are being pulled towards new openings and new possibilities.

It might be helpful to think of Shift 2 as an invitation to step into your individual self where, for the first time, you'll be able to recognize future possibilities that are beckoning to you. You'll discover that the way to the greater sense of meaning and connection that you long for is inward, that is, into your *self,* not out or over or beyond or above, but right into the heart of the matter, right into the felt lack or emptiness you have been experiencing. One man put it this way:

> *The moment I accepted that this was where I was standing in my life—with these feelings of total emptiness—it was like coming to a place where I felt that maybe it was okay to stop and look around. What I then realized was that I'd been running from a strange sound in the distance that I did not understand and then, when I came to a resting place I discovered it was actually somebody calling my*

name. And it was good news, not bad! It was an opening, not a closing down.

New Depths and the Unknown

As you begin to move into Shift 2, you may sense the possibility for something new even as you register the presence of unknown and threatening depths. Strong fears might be aroused here because you'll be encountering the familiar ways of being that, up to now, have protected you from experiences you could not accept or digest. It wouldn't be unusual to feel like you are walking into the place of pain and disconnection, loneliness and emptiness that you have worked your entire life to heal or avoid. As one woman would put it after completing the seven shifts for the first time in her life:

> *In retrospect I can say that the only place I could possibly go with all this was to throw myself into it, allowing the feelings I was so afraid to be in, I kept thinking of the Uncle Remus stories my mother read me when I was a child, especially that one about Brer Rabbit telling Brer Fox, "whatever you do, please don't throw me in the brier-patch." And then it turns out, that's exactly where Brer Rabbit wants to be. I think about that now, that what at first looked like the proverbial brier-patch is actually my salvation, exactly where I want to be, no matter how it might have looked at first.*

Many of us have initially experienced the opening of Shift 2 through sensations or images suggestive of open wounds, black holes, and bottomless, dark, swampy, murky places—or brier patches like in the above recollection of the Joel Chandler Harris stories of Brer Rabbit. No wonder, then, that our first impulses would be to recoil in fear or repulsion. Is it any wonder that we find it difficult to understand how these same forbidding images might be the promising and life-giving forces that are pulling us into our greater depths? Dark though this opening might at first seem, we are soon to see the constructive roles they play in calling us to radical change, where we will understand and relate to this dark emptiness in a brand new way.

Swamps and Tender Spots

In his essay *Walking*, Henry David Thoreau expressed his love of swamps. He said, "Swamps...are the tender places on the Earth's surface...Hope and the future for me are...the quaking swamps...the jewel that dazzles me...I often think I should like to have this fertile spot under my windows..." Thoreau's affection and respect for the value of swamps runs counter to popular opinion, where they generally evoke a sense of dark foggy dampness, both frightening and mysterious, where slimy things reside, hidden and waiting in mucky, murky wetness. Naturalists, while not necessarily embracing swamps as passionately as Thoreau, have discovered and documented the diversity and fertility of swamps. They've explored the important roles these wetland places serve the life of our planet, being as fecund, creative, and nurturing as they are seemingly inhospitable to humans. It seems a worthy metaphor for us here. Like Thoreau's swamp, the place we enter in Shift 2 is a *tender spot,* a place where we are vulnerable because it is here that we are open to growing into the unknown, into a place fertile with unknown possibility.

Our tender spots are areas within our present self-and-world structure where we are most open to new depth and open to the world. As such, it is in these spots where we can be most affected by pleasure and pain. For example, when we open ourselves to others, we open ourselves to experiencing a wide range of feelings, from love, acceptance, connection and affirmation, to rejection, abandonment, mistreatment and betrayal. In our development as human beings, most of us have covered over or distanced ourselves from these tender spots, as determined by a combination of our innate capacity for handling painful or frightening experiences, to our learned ability to stay open and receptive to the unknown.

As we are drawn into new depths that are unfamiliar to us, our tender spots are awakened. With that opening, unresolved hurt, fear and threatening possibilities can also be stirred. We often move into these tender spots without knowing how we're going to handle ourselves. The pull to unknown depths arouses the tender places from our earlier life of being helpless and vulnerable. The extent to which we felt safe or traumatized during those times will determine, to a large part, how we interpret and handle these reawakened tender spots.

Maybe we experienced much pain as infants, after which we found ways to defend ourselves from ever experiencing such pain again. For example, a man in his mid-forties realized that although he was quite successful in his career as an author and speaker he felt he had been living in a very small box and always held himself back in some ways he could not at first identify or recall.

With growing frustration and pressure to break through his perceived limitations, he felt pulled down into new depths, into his tender spots, where he discovered a more authentic and creative inner voice. However, before he could fully claim this voice as his own, and bring it out into the world through his work, he experienced overwhelming anxiety. His childhood fears of an angry and hypercritical father were reawakened. In response, he temporarily retreated back into the small box he'd found, so many years in the past, where he could protect himself from the raging beast (his father). In the process, of course, he abandoned his own growing authority and personal depth.

When our tender spots are recalled to our lives, our first response is frequently to retreat to those defended fortresses that have protected us in the past. Shaky and uncomfortable as those defenses might be, we tell ourselves, anything is better than having to face this brand new set of fears.

Not everyone will have experienced such early fear. Nor will we all have created such defended fortresses to protect ourselves. Those of us who grew up in more supportive environments will likely have less difficulty accepting our experiences of helplessness and entering the tender spots where we might find the path to our true self.

In Shift 2, we are faced with the dilemma of accepting the fact that in order to move on and grow we will need to give up our familiar way of operating in the world before we have gained any confidence about our new way of relating to the world. As we let go of our usual way of relating and accept our felt lack, we come into our own unique experience without the familiar tools and meanings that previously linked us to the world. We climb into a deeper sense of our separateness and individuality in order to discover this new depth in ourselves–the only place where we can fulfill our longing.

Ironically, as we first enter this new depth, we often feel more separate and alone than ever, in addition to feeling helpless. Our tender spots are, after all, often associated with feelings of being alone and vulnerable. No wonder that the experience of exploring our tender spots and coming into greater depth are often, at least initially, associated with a sense of insecurity, pain, loneliness and fear.

Given all this, as you enter Shift 2, it will be quite natural for you to think, "If this experience is ultimately good news, how can it feel so wrong, so frightening, so counter to what feels like healing or growth?" The long and the short of it is that this tender spot is where you feel incomplete since it is where your usual way of being is letting you down. The very vulnerability you are now experiencing is letting you down not in the way of disappointing you but in terms of receiving you into new and yet to be explored depths of your being.

The Sub-Shifts: Moving Towards Acceptance

If we were to closely scrutinize Shift 2 in slow motion, we'd discover four sub-shifts that prepare the path into new openings within ourselves. The sub-shifts can be very subtle and difficult to identify. Becoming aware of them can make it more possible for you to see where and how you are supporting or blocking your progress towards new openings.

The four Sub-Shifts of Shift 2 are:

Sub-Shift A. Experiencing Your Limit: Struggling and failing; Coming to the end of your rope; knowing you are at your limit.

Sub-Shift B. Acceptance of Not Knowing What to Do: Accepting your helplessness.

Sub-Shift C. Showing Up: Having a readiness to respond spontaneously to whatever comes next; being available to the pull of the felt lack and the experience of emptiness.

Sub-Shift D. Entering an Opening to New Depth: Allowing yourself to dwell within.

Sub-Shift A: Experiencing Your Limit

In this first sub-shift we come to a felt awareness of our limits. It is here that our sense of lack is most intense, that is, when we know that there is nothing to do and nowhere to go. We know that whatever we have tried is not working in this situation and that it will not work. People describe this sub-shift with various statements such as: "I'm up against a wall; I've come to the end of my rope; I'm cornered and there's no way out; nothing is working; it's pointless and futile."

The most important aspect of this sub-shift is that we come to know we are helpless in a concrete, *felt* way. This kind of knowing is not abstract, theoretical or speculative, but rather through exhausting all means of trying to change how we feel, we experience our limits and the hollowness of any further efforts or actions.

Struggling as Engagement

Though it does so against our will, our struggling brings us to the end of our ability to affect change. It is here that we find our limits. Through our futile struggling we recognize we are no longer able to create our lives according to our ideas and hopes. We are unable to move ahead, unable to move forward with meaningful plans and relationships. Our existing ways of being and coping come up short, because in fact they are short–short of the depth we are being called into. We feel we have exhausted all possibilities.

Paradoxically our struggle serves to increase our awareness of our lack. As strange as it might seem, each time you fail to overcome this felt lack, you move toward a more direct relationship with it. You begin to experience more directly the presence of your lack as well as your helplessness to ameliorate it. In Tolstoy's essay, *A Confession,* he describes a dream that illuminates how our struggles increase our awareness of the lack and eventually reveal our powerlessness to overcome it:

> *I see that I am lying on a bed. I am neither comfortable, nor uncomfortable. I am lying on my back. But I start to think about whether or not I am comfortable and it seems to me that my legs are a bit awkward; I do not know whether it is that they are too short or that they are uneven. I shift my legs and at the same time I begin to think about the way I am lying and what I am lying on, things which had not entered my head until now. And looking at my bed I see that I am lying on some plaited rope supports that are attached to the sides of the bed. My feet are resting on one of the supports, my calves on another and my legs are uncomfortable. I somehow know that these supports can be moved. Moving one of my legs I push away the furthest support beneath my feet. I presume that this will be better. But I have pushed it too far and want to rescue it with my legs, and this movement causes yet another support, beneath my calves, to fall off and my calves are left dangling. I move my whole body in order to adjust my position and am quite certain that this will settle the matter. But with this movement still more of the supports slip and move away beneath me and I can see that things are getting worse: the whole lower part of my body is*

slipping and hanging down, and my feet do not reach the ground. I am only supported on the upper half of my back and I start to feel not just uncomfortable but terrified of something, only at this point do I ask myself the thing that has not yet entered my head. I ask myself: where am I and what am I lying on? I begin looking around and before anywhere else I look beneath me, where my body is dangling and in the direction where I feel I am bound to fall very soon, I look below and I cannot believe my eyes. I am at a height not just of, say, an extremely tall tower or mountain, but I am at a height such as I could never have imagined.

I cannot even discern whether I can see anything there below, in the bottomless abyss over which I am hanging and into which I am being drawn. My heart contracts and I feel terrified. It is dreadful to look down there. I feel that if I look down I will immediately slip from the last support and perish. I do not look, but not looking is still worse because I am thinking about what is going to happen to me when I slip from the last support. And I feel that I am losing my last bit of strength through terror, and that my back is slowly slipping lower and lower. Another moment and I will fall off. And then I have a thought: perhaps it is not real. It is a dream. I will wake up. I try to wake up and cannot. What can I do, what can I do?

As we attempt to adjust ourselves and our lives we find that our situation or condition is more profound and we are more helpless than even we first imagined. We become increasingly aware that the ground we are standing on, what has been supporting us, is very thin indeed, or as Tolstoy expresses, not really there at all.

It is difficult to remember at this point that the pull of your felt lack is a pull toward fulfillment of your free-floating longing, but difficult as it might seem, we must accept this on faith and move forward.

Sub-Shift B: Acceptance of Not Knowing What to Do

Our response to knowing there is nothing to do or nowhere to go is decisive in determining whether we are cooperating with or stymieing the forces that are pulling us on behalf of Deep Change. If we are to respond fruitfully at this often tension-filled threshold, we have no choice but to accept our present discomforts and face our sense of lack with openness, and without grasping for explanations and meanings.

Moving into this Sub-Shift hinges on the distinction between resignation and acceptance, and it's essential that we learn to discern between them when we are experiencing one or the other. While they can look very much alike, they are worlds apart. In fact, I mention this here because it is a common sticking point. While relatively easy to understand and apply, it does require careful attention. Until you discern the difference, it can be virtually impossible to move forward with any certainty.

The Latin origin of the word "acceptance" is *acceptare* (E.Partridge, 1958), which means "to receive." This receptiveness depends on our being vulnerable and available; otherwise, we literally cannot fully receive what's being offered. Think of acceptance as coming to you as an open invitation to respond to the pull of your felt lack or emptiness.

By contrast, the Latin origin of the word "resignation" is *resignare* (E.Partridge, 1958), which means to "annul or abdicate." To be resigned is to withdraw from the challenge. It is a passive *giving up* or an *abdication.*

When we respond with resignation to the call of Shift 2, we are essentially saying to ourselves: If I can't be in charge, if I am unable to create my life as I wish and thus be in control of my desired change, if I can't make myself who I want to be, or make my life and my world the way I want it to be, then forget it. Why bother? What's the point? I give up. We are withdrawing from our place of lack and abandoning our tender spot. Essentially, when we are in resignation we are still trying to find ways to exert some control over our experience, whether it is to explain it, hide from it, or even end it.

In order to avoid being capsized by resignation, it is important to distinguish between the actual felt lack and the stories and meanings we attribute to them. These experiences and the stories we attribute to them are intricately intertwined–and our stories can be so convincing! After all, we have created them, consciously or not, in order to have credible explanations for why we are feeling as we do.

For example, what might come up around our tender spot is a feeling of being alone and exiled from the world. Rather than feeling this directly, we might make up a story to explain or rationalize it. We might tell ourselves, "The reason I feel so apart from the world is because I am unlovable and not a worthwhile person." Over time, you may have disproved your story many times over during your better moments. You know your story isn't true. However, now you are in the process of Deep Change and you've come to the place of your tender spot and experience your sense of lack. Once again the same old stories about being unlovable arise. To the extent that you resist or succumb to this story, you are in resignation. "Ah," a part of you says, "Why struggle? I'm a failure, just as I always feared. Why fight what is so obvious!"

What's the alternative? It's to look upon your story as just a story, seeing and observing it, neither fighting it nor believing it. Stories are, after all, simply created expressions, fictional accounts of experiences made up of observations and reflections based on limited knowledge we possessed at the time of that experience. As we gain greater knowledge the stories we have created in the past will prove to be only tiny pieces of much bigger pictures.

Gaining this perspective on our stories is probably going to require considerable practice, so later in this chapter a series of questions are provided as guides to help you separate your stories from the felt experiences of your tender spot. Remember that we are looking at Shift 2 in very slow motion through the Sub-Shifts because this can help us see if we are moving towards acceptance and opening, or holding ourselves back in resignation, a disguise for trying to stay in control.

For now, moving into this Sub-Shift, we become able to accept our felt lack as it is, on its own terms, so to speak, without overlays and interpretations on our part. We come nakedly face to face with our tender spot, and hold ourselves open and receptive to what we know not.

Sub-Shift C: Showing Up

When standing openly at the threshold of your tender spot, you realize that the emptiness or felt lack that you are now exposed to is not a vacuum or a nothingness; rather, it has a definite and palpable presence, a presence with a pull–a pull into unknown depths within yourself. And in a mode of accepting just where you are, you are showing up, so to speak, to this pull. You are available to this pull, which originates from other than your familiar way of doing and being. Your accepting mode makes you receptive to movements and forces not under your usual control, and you respond spontaneously to the pull of your tender spot.

Sub-Shift D: Entering an Opening to New Depth

As we respond spontaneously to the pull of our tender spot, we find ourselves entering and dwelling *within* our tender spot, which turns out to be an opening into new territories, depths and possibilities within our individual self.

Recall that your felt lack is *felt,* meaning that it is not an idea or story or theory, but is palpable. While not necessarily a physical sensation per se, it can register as a *felt* experience. So when we become available to the pull of this opening, we are drawn into and towards the inner felt experience of the lack or emptiness. Our attention comes into an opening, a space within ourselves that is not predetermined with meanings and stories, it is more of an empty, unknown space, but one that draws us into our self, nonetheless. Although it may feel foreign, it belongs to us, it is our very own tender spot, our opening to fertile depths.

It's important to realize that as we give ourselves over to the spontaneous pull of the tender spot, we may find that we initially recoil and move back out of this place. It can feel dark, murky, and swampy. We already know that there is nowhere else we can go, but we may still jump away. Eventually, we need to exercise our "accepting awareness" so that we can build tolerance for this unknown place and begin to look around and become more accustomed to our experience. In short, the movement of this Sub-Shift requires that we develop the capacity to dwell within our tender spot, where we will find, in Shift 3, the Unraveling, as we continue to be drawn down into unknown personal depths.

The following is a description of the experience of the four Sub-Shifts from a woman I was seeing in my therapy practice:

I felt an increasing pressure around a sense of failure. Professionally, I had always thought that I would do something, write something original and important. Whenever I read or heard someone in my field present original research I felt envious and even bitter, "I could do that."

But lately, this feeling of failure, of not living up to my expectations has grown stronger and I can't seem to ignore it. As I let myself eventually just feel this sense of failure I became aware of a longing to find my own voice, to be true to my own knowing. And then I began to feel how this longing registers in my experience, I started to describe it. I became aware of the sense of a dark hole in the area of my heart. As I just allowed this dark hole to be there and I with it, I found that I was pulled into it. I felt that I was in a small, cramped, dark and narrow tube. I felt that I was in there because I was being punished. I was all alone and afraid and angry. I thought, "I am not going to stay here. Why should I? Why should I be punished?"

So I refused to stay there, only to eventually feel the sense of failure and bitterness once more.

As this woman let herself be pulled into her felt lack, she entered into an opening to a deeper part of herself, an opening that would eventually lead her to her authentic creativity, which she longed for. But as we see here, as she first entered that opening, that tender spot, she associated it with some sense of being abandoned and punished. We can assume this experience has some connection to her past, but that is not really important at this point. What matters is that she become increasingly aware that the strong feelings and meanings she associates with her tender spot are not literally true, they are meanings aroused by a "story" she has related to the experience of being in her own tender spot. This awareness will help her develop the ability to reside within her tender spot while not being fooled by the meanings, to learn to tolerate them without reacting to them so that she can dwell within the opening through which she can be available to the pull into a deeper and truer self.

Teasing Out Our Stories

Developing the ability to tease out our stories and meanings from the actual felt experiences in our tender spots takes practice, but is practice very well worth it. Our ability to allow ourselves to dwell within these often threatening and unknown places in ourselves while holding steady and not reacting, will be what opens us to our birthright of rich potentials and transformational change.

The following six questions may help you become more aware of the stories and meanings wedded to your experience of lack, emptiness and longing. Set aside some time when you will be uninterrupted by outside distractions so that you can familiarize yourself with these questions. Be prepared to either write down your answers or say them into a tape recorder. If you wish, consider working with another person and telling them your answers.

You'll recognize the first two questions from Shift 1: The Unsettling:

Question #1: What is the experience you are having that you presently want to change? Example: "I am feeling abandoned and unloved. I am feeling hollow and helpless."

Question #2: How would you feel differently if you were able to change your experience in the way that you wish? (Your answer to this question may begin to reveal your longing.) Example: "I'd feel more in control of my life, more hopeful. I'd have a sense of belonging, of being wanted and with a sense of purpose. I'd like to be in a fulfilling relationship."

Question #3: What will you experience if you accept that you are unable to make your desired changes? (Your answers may reveal a combination of your felt lack and your stories.) Example: "I'd feel like a huge failure, weak, doomed, lost and utterly alone."

Question #4: What does it mean to you that you would have this experience...that you are in this situation? What does it mean about you? About the world? (Your answers may reveal your judgments about being helpless in the face of your felt lack.) Example: "I've blown it. The world is a sham, nothing's real. What's the point, I'll never be happy. Things will only get worse. I've never been allowed to have what I really want. I'm feeling totally unworthy. Life is so unfair!"

Question #5: Observe your story lines. Ask yourself what aspects of your experience you are resisting. What are you judging? What have you decided is not acceptable? (Note: Let your stories just be there, like tall tales. Just witness them with the eye of an unattached observer. Then turn your attention to what you are actually feeling.)

Example: "I'm feeling empty and disconnected, sad. I'm feeling scared and isolated. There's a sense of grief and shame."

Question #6: Let yourself experience these feelings in your body, in your muscles and bones and insides. Where do these feelings seem to draw you? Can you describe them? What sensations are you the most present with? What gives you the sense that you are having a particular feeling? How is it registering in your being? Example: "My jaw is tight, like a vice. My heart feels sore, almost burning. I feel raw, wounded, endlessly hurt. In a dark hole all by myself."

Some people report quite different sensations, often described as *spaccy-ness*: "I'm floating in I don't know what... spinning, nauseous. I feel a tingling in my body, a big, gnawing weight in the pit of my stomach."

It can be very difficult to just allow yourself to dwell within these feelings. You may find it supportive to remember that what you are experiencing is in response to your longing for greater depth and connection with yourself and with life. Remind yourself that these feelings are telling you that your old familiar ways no longer work for you. If fears arise, as they may, see if you can observe them, and for just a few seconds bring your attention into that sense of fear and describe what you are noticing.

Where are you in your body? Is your attention on your gut, your face, your chest, your shoulders? How large are these feelings? Can you describe what it looks like? (Perhaps you can draw a picture.) What other qualities can you notice and describe?

The Search for Meaning

The series of questions above are intended to help you experience and describe your responses to your felt lack while not taking them literally. It is a tall order, but again, it is ultimately a most rewarding accomplishment.

When anxiety takes hold of us, our first reaction is often to look for an explanation of why we are feeling this way. What does it mean? Western psychology offers a way of looking at the past, to hopefully relate present feelings or perceptions to early wounds. Following such a system, we often devote much attention to what is causing such strong reactions. *What past trauma am I reliving through this present experience*? Such information can be helpful in gauging the extent to which we accept ourselves or have compassion for who we are. But in and of themselves, such analyses usually can't help us dwell with our present, felt responses. In fact, such explanations may provide little more than stories to keep us in the safety of our uncomfortably familiar lives.

To move forward, we need to understand our felt responses as calls that are beckoning to us from a world of future possibility. We need to educate ourselves about the meanings of our felt responses so that we can suffer (allow) them, and not be fooled by their misguided warnings. Then, even as our experiences of them seem to foretell certain disaster, we can hold steady, confident that there is a new form of fulfillment close at hand.

One man in a workshop kept repeating that his sense of meaninglessness was very real and terrifying. As he asked himself the above questions, it became clear how little he actually knew about his felt terror. Inside he was like Chicken Little, darting around exclaiming, "This is terrible, this is terrible. The sky is falling."

After asking himself these questions, he watched himself running in circles around his own terror. The more he allowed himself to observe this pattern the less he felt a captive of his own panic. This made it possible for him to begin to attend to his actual felt response. Here is what he described:

> *I feel out of control. There's something I cannot face, some horrible truth. I feel it everywhere, especially my chest where I can hardly get a full breath.*

As he let himself breathe into his chest more deeply and gently, he became aware that his sense of meaninglessness meant that he was insignificant. He said:

I do not matter one iota. I will disappear as though I never existed.

Again, as he became aware of his story as just a story, he gradually let himself enter and describe his felt lack:

I'm squeezed into a tightness in my chest. I'm all alone and afraid...of what I don't know. But if I relax I feel that I will not exist.

As he allowed himself to just dwell within the tightness in his chest, he then reported:

I'm floating in an empty space in my chest. The space is getting larger and I feel very sad and somewhat relieved, maybe even a bit peaceful. I'm not sure, it is not anything familiar.

Having entered into his felt lack, free of the associated stories and felt responses, he was then able to dwell within what turned out to be an opening to new depth where he felt neither resistance nor the need to grasp for meanings. He was no longer a captive of his terror.

The Power of Accepting Awareness

We humans tend to underestimate the power of our accepting awareness. I've often heard people say, "What good could that possibly do?" when I suggest they simply observe their story or dwell within their experience. We are so habituated to rolling up our sleeves and seeing what can be done to *fix* what is happening that we cannot even imagine another way. Surprisingly, when we are finally able to be in this state of accepting awareness, we start to let go of the tension we've been exerting to keep these stories and feelings at bay. We discover ourselves opening to new depths within ourselves and to a greater freedom for expressing who we are.

As we move through the sub-shifts of the Opening, we accept our felt lack on its own terms. The bonds that seem to weave together the feelings we are having with the meanings and stories we attribute to them begin to unravel. As we dwell within our felt lack, we allow ourselves to feel the lack itself, free of any circle of meaning wound around it. We experience the felt lack's innate open-endedness and can be there within this space. Once this occurs, the habitual meanings we may be holding around the felt lack relaxes, leaving space for something new and unfamiliar to enter into our lives, taking us to new depths.

One author, Sylvia Ashton-Warner, suggests that there is a point at which we let go of the stories by which we define our lives; abandoning ourselves in this way we surrender to the creative process: "Self-forgetfulness in creativity can lead to self-transcendence." We not only create but we change through surrendering ourselves to the unknown.

Keep in mind that this movement within Shift 2 is not necessarily swift, or tidy. Rather, it is more likely to follow a three-steps-forward-and-two-back rhythm; we get caught up in our stories, become aware of them, let go and open again; then, as new stories and meanings arise, we get scared and confused again. We repeat what we have learned about observing and describing our stories and the new fears fall away.

In time, as we follow these rhythms, we find ourselves dwelling with greater ease within our felt lack, allowing ourselves to be pulled down into our own personal depths where the unraveling dance of resisting and letting go continues to draw us towards our future.

The Power of Curiosity

Awareness of our longing, of the pull towards something outside us, can provide the emotional room to be curious about our experience. This same curiosity can be a helpful companion on your journey of Deep Change.

Curiosity is a state of mind wherein we tend to accept that there is something we don't know and so are open to the mystery it presents. But beware of the impulse to control and explain that wears the disguise of curiosity. Fruitful, genuine curiosity is a wide-awake and open-ended wonderment. It is a supportive sister to acceptance and receptivity.

Stay with feelings of awe and wonder as you go through this shift. Allow these, the inner muses of curiosity, to guide you and they will bring you into the state of acceptance you are seeking.

Help With Despair

The philosopher Kierkegaard said that despair is always over something. It is resisting something. If you are in a state of deep despair or resignation as you work with the Unsettling, you may very well be "despairing over your despair." This is not uncommon; it involves a judgment on your part that your state of resignation is wrong, weak, bad, sick, etc. Remember that acceptance is the key to supporting your opening to new depths, and that this may require that you let yourself feel whatever you are feeling, be it resignation, despair, or anything else, without trying to change, judge, or withdraw from it. This is not easy since your resignation may be accompanied by a determination to not open. At the same time, you may encounter, deep within you, something that allows you to dwell with your despair, knowing that in doing so you will paradoxically create an opening, a movement towards acceptance.

Try closing your eyes, breathing deeply and gently, and then allow yourself to notice all the sensations and experiences that you associate with what you would call despair; see if you can observe and describe what you are aware of, paying attention to areas in your body where you seem to be drawn as you focus on sensations and feelings.

If you feel numb, let your self attend to what it's like to not be feeling anything. Notice the stories and meanings you have about your numbness and let them just be there in your awareness. Our greatest torments at these times arise out of the meanings we give to our experience of lack, emptiness and helplessness, and the paralyzing tension that we exert to ward them off. But judging these meanings and trying to change them will only perpetuate further resignation.

Be aware, however, that allowing yourself to be present with your despair is not a passive state. It is not despairing over your despair. It is a courageous gesture, one that requires alert and receptive attention. It can also be a very good time to seek support and guidance from a trusted friend or professional, because it can be extremely difficult to learn to dwell with despair and re-signation on our own.

Most Important

Be very gentle and patient with yourself as you move through this shift, observing and dwelling in your experience. Even though things may feel very rough and hopeless, the more you can soften and relax around the places you are most hurt, afraid and tender, the more mercifully you will be guided and welcomed into the openings around which they hover, openings to your promise and birthright for a deeper joining with yourself and with life. The Unraveling, which is the next shift we'll be looking at, reveals the dismantling of self-and-world structures which are the basis of our stories, and it is from this point on that new worlds open up to us.

...If only we knew
as the carver knew, how the flaws
in the wood led his searching chisel
to the very core,

We would smile too
and not need faces immobilized
by fear and the weight of things undone.

When we fight with our failing
we ignore the entrance to the shrine itself
and wrestle with the guardian,
fierce figure on the side of good.

And as we fight
our eyes are hooded with grief
and our mouths are dry with pain.

If only we could give ourselves
to the blows of the carvers hands,
the lines in our faces would be
the trace lines of rivers

feeding the sea
where voices meet, praising the features
of the mountain and the cloud and the sky.

Our faces would fall away
until we, growing younger toward death
every day, would gather all our flaws in celebration

to merge with them perfectly,
impossibly, wedded to our essence
full of silence from the carver's hands.
—David Whyte

Footholds

Remember...

- You are feeling your sense of lack and emptiness because a new possibility is beckoning.
- Your felt lack is where you will discover your tender spot.
- Your tender spot is where you may find pain and hurt and a sense of failure, but it is also the opening to your own unknown depths.
- You're helpless in terms of your familiar tools and ways of coping.
- Allowing yourself to dwell within your tender spot is not passive or weak, but is courageous and requires active, alert, receptive and patient attention.

Also remember to...

- Let yourself become aware of how you are judging your experience of lack and helplessness.

What meanings or stories are you are attributing to it?

- What aspects of your experience are you resisting? What associations do you have with being vulnerable and alone?
- Practice describing what you actually feel. Notice where your lack resides in your body, and how you experience its presence. Describe what you notice out loud to someone, draw a picture of it, write it down.
- Let yourself float in your sense of lack or emptiness, noticing its currents and changes without manipulating them or analyzing them.
- See if you can sense your longing for greater depth. Attend to its pull in your body.
- Cultivate curiosity.
- Find someone who can help you to build your capacity to dwell with your experience, including teachers of meditation or other contemplative arts.

When water gets caught in habitual whirlpools,
dig a way out through the bottom
to the ocean. There is a secret medicine
given only to those who hurt so hard
they can't hope.
The hopers would feel slighted if they knew.

- From The Essential Rumi

Shift 3: The Unraveling

You experience the Unraveling as you are *pulled down* into your own personal depths, the depths that first began opening to you in Shift 2. The Unraveling can occur swiftly or can take place over a period of months or even years. It's important to understand at this point that as you enter this shift you have passed a kind of *point of no return* in your journey of Deep Change. As you let yourself dwell within your felt lack in Shift 2, the downward pull of Shift 3 will take hold. The force of this pull is now stronger than your personal will.

With the unraveling of your familiar way of being in the world, a relaxing occurs. And in this relaxing there is a freeing up of the life-energy that you have exerted, for perhaps much of your life, keeping you out of personal depths that had seemed to be threatening you. When you bring your allowing awareness to the Unraveling, it becomes a powerful life-giving force; it penetrates through to the truth, liberating the life that up to now was captured within what is now an outgrown need to ward off that truth.

For some of us, the Unraveling can be a most challenging shift, one we'll resist with all our might. However, the more you understand the bigger picture in which this shift is embedded, the less likely you are to resist; this is a principle you'll find to be true throughout the journey into your personal depths. *How* you respond to the Unraveling experience can either ease your way or increase your struggle.

It is here in the Unraveling that our allowing awareness serves to relax or loosen (*unravel*) the intricately woven tapestry of our perceptions about who we are and what our world is about. During the course of our lives, from conception through birth, then into infancy, childhood, adolescence and adulthood, we encounter the pressure to change many times over. At each such juncture, we let go of something we have valued up until that moment; by doing so we provide the space within our consciousness to allow for something new. Each growth phase is ideally accompanied by an ever more intricate self identity and world view. Now, as adults facing the growth of Deep Change, and immersed in the Unraveling, we must once again witness the dismantling of our self-created identity, one in which we have invested so much for so many years. We may well ask, why are we now being urged to let go of what we have spent a lifetime building?

The answer to that question isn't simple. Change and growth at this time in our lives is not just voluntary.

It is as if we are answering a call coming from outside us, responding to that which longs for us. As we outgrow our current ways of being, we long for deeper meaning, a deeper sense of belonging, which is characteristic of our movement into greater *depth* within ourselves. What's no longer meaningful to us *must* fall away, yet even knowing this our reflex is to hold on, to cling to the known and familiar.

Though we are out-growing our present inner structure, we resist letting go of that which has provided a place of safety for us. Doing so might well be compared with the fear we must encounter as babies leaving the safety of the womb. Familiarity can have a powerful hold on us, even when it is uncomfortable, making it difficult to let go of even the most negative or self-destructive structures.

Many Varieties of Meaning

As our self-and-world-structure is subjected to the Unraveling, we begin experiencing a wide variety of subjective events. These may include experiences we once visited and then repressed, even ones from which we recoiled in horror or disgust. It may include aspects of ourselves that we've never before recognized. We might uncover untapped potentials of creativity and alternate ways of relating, or memories of past experiences that we were unable to digest at the time they occurred.

Some people encounter subjective experiences that are archetypal in nature, that is, belonging to a *collective consciousness* of which they are a part. Such experiences usually arise from cultural or historical contexts, rather than solely from individual life. This might include memories associated with the experience of being a member of a particular ethnic group or a group that played an important part in history. For example, a person of Jewish origin might *relive* experiences of the holocaust even though they hadn't actually experienced the actual holocaust firsthand. Or, if your ancestors were early immigrants you might imagine revisiting an area that had once been a famous pioneering village, and find yourself immersed in events that occurred there hundreds of years before. It can be helpful to keep such possibilities in mind, realizing that as we enter the deepest parts of our being we might discover *memories* that have their origins not in our direct, firsthand experience but from an awareness that has been carried across many generations.

The Allowing Awareness

You'll remember that in the last chapter we addressed the role our *allowing awareness* plays in opening to our own depths. In the Unraveling, this allowing awareness continues to be essential. Here, when we encounter an experience, feeling or belief that is painful or difficult to look at, our first impulse may be to turn away from it. But as we already know, this reaction only creates more tension, prolonging the period we must struggle.

When we bring our allowing awareness into the center of an experience that we've encountered in our own depths, the meanings we have previously attributed to that experience *relax,* just as might happen with the loosened weavings of a woven tapestry. This loosening is the essence of the Unraveling, with old structures and old perceptions of our lives literally and figuratively coming apart, ultimately freeing us to experience ourselves and the world around us in a different way. As one woman put it, "I can remember how afraid I was at first, as I seemed to be dropping deeper and deeper into a place that was definitely strange and forbidding...like some dark cave, with the monsters that awoke me in terror when I was a little child. There was no way I was going to believe that I was supposed to go there, but I did go there anyway. Then, as I allowed myself to just drop into that place, and settle in as best I could, a shift occurred...and what I had at first thought were monsters became my allies, not monsters at all...nor was any of it so frightening anymore. I became more and more comfortable in this place, drawing strength from it rather than feeling I had to fear it or avoid it...actually feeling more myself."

As you will recall from Shift 2, most of the fears we experience in our own depths grow out of the *meanings* we have assigned to our experiences. Those meanings are judgments determined by our own perceived values, with the degrees of acceptability or unacceptability we've attributed to those experiences. Those attributed meanings and judgments prevent us from fully feeling the experience for itself, free of our attributions.

This dynamic of judgment and attribution not only affects how we relate to ourselves, it also affects how we relate to others. For example, you may encounter someone who appears to be very angry. Your first impulse might be to withdraw, react angrily in return, or avoid any future contact. But if somehow you were given the opportunity to get to know this person, you might discover that he or she is actually very frightened and therefore quick to shove the world away. With further contact, you discover this person feels helpless and hurt. If you are able to hang in there with them, without *deciding* ahead of time what is true about him or her, then you may become aware of many more facets of their character, each one taking you closer to their true nature. In this way, we expand our capacity to relate to others and ourselves.

In the Unraveling, we need to learn to *hang in there* with ourselves, which means to *be with what is* rather than allowing our judgments or limited perceptions to dominate. Let's say a person lives his life believing and feeling that he is giving and generous. As a matter of fact, evidence might show that his major life choices were guided primarily by his belief in his own generosity and need to help. Then one day, perhaps during a crisis, he becomes painfully aware that his apparent generosity is, in reality, motivated by a self-centeredness that he had not previously realized.

At first he reacts with horror and indignation, defending his generosity as genuine and selfless. But gradually, he just looks at this *truth,* feels it, sees it and allows it to just be there. Suddenly he recalls a painful memory about his parents telling him how selfish he was anytime he tried to assert his own needs. As he relives this painful memory, which he had kept at bay by his giving to others to "prove" he was not what his parents said, he suddenly realizes that the meaning of his *self-centeredness* was that he felt unloved and that he was a "bad person" for making personal demands. With this realization, he could now separate that particular meaning and judgment from his desire to attend to his own needs.

At this point, it was just *simply true* that he had needs and desires that sometimes came first for him. As he allowed himself to be aware that this was simply true for him, without the overlay of meanings and judgments, he felt a great relief. And paradoxically, in his new freedom, he experienced a more genuine caring and enjoyment of giving.

In this example we can see how the loosening power of his allowing awareness revealed hidden, successive meanings within his own depths, meanings he had avoided for years. Disclosing these layers of meaning eventually brought him into a more real relationship with himself, and therefore, a more genuine relationship with the world. While he continued to be a giving and generous person, he now felt good about himself, worthy of expressing his needs and having them met.

When we come to the place where we can allow a truth about ourselves to just be, we usually feel relief, like the man in my example above. The truth feels good, but there is also an actual relaxing, the setting down of a burden, the release of a tension that we once believed we had to uphold in order to fend off the truth.

During the Unraveling, the point is not to go on a mining expedition to uncover every nook and cranny of our deeper selves. Rather, it is to be with whatever presents itself in a way that allows us to be more fully available to the pull of our longing. It is so easy to be captured by the content of our experiences and all that we associate with them. Many of us get so caught up in particular events from our past—such as the tragic death of a loved one or severe emotional or physical abuse—that we live our whole lives in context with that event. We may spend thousands of dollars in an effort to forget something horrible that's happened to us, or we simply become immersed in the darkness of that experience, without ever asking what it *means* to us or what it might tell us about ourselves.

How ironic it is that the source of our own suffering is in the meaning we attribute to our experiences! And it is doubly ironic that our liberation might be found in the seemingly simple act of becoming aware of those same attributed meanings.

Truth of Your Experience

What I refer to as "the truth of an experience" is what we experience when we are free of the habitual meanings we have attributed to that experience. When we just allow ourselves to experience the truth of an event, memory, or feeling in our lives, we allow it to become an unknown, free of our deciding what it means. It becomes itself, without our coloring and shading. Experiencing the truth in this way *does not mean* that we are experiencing the ultimate truth, that is, Truth with a capital "T." It's important to address this fact since it helps to deflect any fear we might have that when the truth comes out it would prove that we are simply not acceptable people. But the opposite is true. The *meaning* we ourselves assign to our experience is, after all, a great source of our suffering. And the moment we can fully accept this fact, the faster we are able to let the unraveling occur and move towards deeper self-knowing, with a growing sense of individual authenticity and self-appreciation. The anecdote in the following section will hopefully shed further light on this process.

Stuck in a Tight Spot

The power of terror in the Unraveling should not be ignored, for it is our fear that gets us stuck. That said, let there be no doubt of how extremely easy it is to be captured by perceived meanings and felt responses as we encounter the unraveling of core beliefs that we closely identify with. It takes tremendous focus and faith to stay the course.

Julie experienced quite a struggle in the Unraveling, which she came into during a critical point in her life when she realized her life had to change. She had recently broken off a romantic relationship and realized that she had been re-creating the same pattern in her choices with men for over ten years. She had come to feel like a mere object for each of them.

In the midst of her crisis, Julie decided to attend a series of extended meditation workshops to help her get to the bottom of this pattern. In the past, she'd had several very enjoyable and fruitful experiences during these workshops and was looking forward to this time.

After several days at the meditation retreat, Julie began to feel a sense of unreality and worthlessness. She could not escape these feelings. Though she tried to argue with them and deny them, her efforts were futile. She continued to feel worthless and empty, certain that her life had no meaning or purpose, and that the truth she had come to was that she was of no value whatsoever.

She struggled for several days, and could not sleep. She even considered leaving the retreat and entering some kind of institutionalized care. Perhaps they could medicate her so that she would not have to feel what she was now feeling. Escaping into some kind of *freak out* mode held more appeal for her than enduring the torture she was experiencing.

This was a silent retreat, so speaking aloud was not allowed, with the exception of individual visits with one of the several guides. Julie's guide kept telling her that he knew what she was experiencing and that she would be okay. This reassurance helped to the extent that she stayed at the retreat, encouraged by some speck of faith that others had gone through similar challenges before her. If this were so, surely she would survive as well.

Julie's unraveling continued, aided by the meditation. She now found only a void concerning everything she had once thought was real and valuable in her life. In her eyes, even her personal identity was void of all reality and meaning. Julie's awareness of *being an object* to herself and to the world had become excruciatingly transparent to her and she now experienced herself as hollow and unreal. As painful as this was she could not return to her former sense of self, because that was now shattered. She described this experience as follows:

"I remembered this cartoon I'd seen a long time ago, as a child, that had really frightened me. This little figure was dancing around on the page and then this giant eraser came out of the sky and simply erased her. That was me being erased. That is how I felt...just erased from the face of the earth with no trace."

For the time being, she was stuck and she was terrified. She could not move forward until she could allow herself to just be with the truth. To do so seemed to be overwhelming. She believed it meant she would not exist. After all, she had lived thus far only as an object in other people's lives. She had not known any other way to be. However, in her descent into her own depths she had come to know a truth beyond that way of being and now her longing for a greater sense of meaning and connection was drawing her. She had passed the point of no return. She could not bear the emptiness and hollowness that she was experiencing.

"After what seemed like three lifetimes," she said, reflecting on a particular moment during the retreat, "I realized that *there really was no way out and so maybe I should just try to let myself be where I was.*" Shortly after she had these thoughts, there was a break in the meditation, and she got up and walked around. When she returned to her meditation pillow, she found that a single fresh rose had been placed upon it. What a surprise! Here she was at a retreat in the middle of the desert and suddenly this beautiful rose had appeared.

She picked the rose up and smelled it, taking what she thought was the first really deep breath she had taken in months. She enjoyed the scent and remembered a dream in which she was smoke drifting to beautiful flute music. As she recalled the dream she rode the flute music, now letting her breath be carried by the scent of the rose into her body and out. She lay the rose down and resumed her meditation position on her pillow. Immediately she returned to the hollowness and dread that she had been experiencing, but this time she was carried swiftly through the emptiness into the next shifts of Deep Change, the Stilling and the Releasing.

As Julie's awareness unraveled her identity as an object for others, she became frozen at a threshold where all she could see on one side was emptiness and hollowness; on the other side, she felt she would surely cease to exist. For the time being, her terror exerted tremendous force to keep her frozen between two untenable realities.

Just before she discovered the rose there had been a moment when she had made the decision to hang in there. She realized there was really no other place to go, so she might as well stay with her experience. In this kind of decision, although subtle and easily missed, there is a little loosening, a little letting go. With the surprise appearance of the rose she had a brief respite, thoroughly enjoying her existence as she inhaled the rose's scent and reveled in the beauty of that moment. At that instant she had allowed her breath to move freely through her.

This time, as she descended into herself again, she found herself carried into the next shift. Because she had some association with herself which was pleasurable—thanks to the rose and reliving the dream—she trusted this new inner movement through the Unraveling and toward the next shift.

Julie's experience serves to highlight the importance of learning ways to bring our allowing awareness into the tight spots we encounter in the Unraveling. Her journey also illustrates how, as we open, even to the tiniest degree, we often discover that help is already there. Remember that you are longed for even as you long. And the larger world of potentiality that is drawing you into its depths will conspire to help you through your difficult times. In the Unraveling, this opening involves bringing our allowing awareness into the heart of whatever we are experiencing.

Breath As Your Ally

Julie's experience also gives us some clues about the importance of our ability to breathe into tight places with which we're confronted. In Shift 2, the Opening, you'll recall how we enter our *being-body*, that is, the whole of our being—body, mind, spirit; we experience feelings of loneliness and separateness because we are entering our own individuality where only we can go. In the Unraveling, we are descending deeper into our being-body and many people describe this experience as being like entering a deep well, a long pit, a tunnel, or a dark column. This sense of a vertical space into which we are entering is often expressed as residing within the center of our being-body, from our chest to the belly or pelvic area. This is the central passage of our breath that we can use for creating an *allowing space* that loosens the tension of our familiar structure.

If you are having a hard time allowing yourself to just be with your experience, first let your awareness go to where your current experience or feelings take you. Where inside yourself are you being pulled? It may be to your head, your shoulders, your chest, belly, pelvis or limbs. Once you've located it, imagine that you are allowing your breath to go to this place. Imagine it surrounding and holding your sensations, feelings and any images that might arise in your mind. If it helps, you can pretend that your breath has a form, such as it did in Julie's story when she recalled the dream of being smoke moving to the sounds of beautiful flute music.

As you allow your breath to move to the area of your body that has drawn your attention, let yourself experience what you are feeling rather than analyzing the feelings or thinking about the story surrounding them. The feelings that now come may be uncomfortable; if they are, dwell with them for a few moments and then describe what these feelings are like for you. Write them down in your journal or tell them to a friend or record them on a small recorder.

It will *not* be helpful to *try* to use your breath to relax or change your experience. As soon as you are trying to change your experience you will be exerting familiar tension that will not serve you. Instead, gently allow your breath to surround your felt experience just as it is, holding the intention of becoming more familiar with it rather than trying to make it go away. Hold its place so that you can get to know these feelings and sensations. This can have the effect of relaxing the tension of meanings that are woven into your experience, and thus create an open and supportive space where you are aware of this experience on its own terms. As we loosen this tension through our allowing awareness, the unraveling of who we thought we were, and of how we related to the world, begins to drop away.

Inner Haiku

Haiku is an excellent way to *describe* our inner experiences, without explanation, analysis or judgment. Haiku, an ancient Japanese literary form, is a poem consisting of only seventeen syllables. The first and third lines contain five syllables and the second line has seven. (Note that the second line is often broken up into two lines, but the total of those two lines is still seven syllables.) Strictly speaking, the traditional Japanese Haiku involves an observation in nature. However, many people find it to be particularly helpful for journaling about Deep Change.

Step One: You may wish to practice this form with an observation from nature. Do not feel that you have to follow the form exactly. After getting comfortable with writing a short verse like this, go on to the next step.

Step Two: Bring your attention into a felt experience within your being-body.

Step Three*:* Using the Haiku form, or your interpretation of it, describe your felt experience and write it down.

Here are two examples:

A red, rising heat
In my chest
so tight
A clenched fist prevails

A hollowness here
in my heart
so vast
Yet I can't get in.

There is no other purpose for describing your experience other than to write the Haiku. This practice will exercise muscles of attention that you need to *dwell within, in an allowing mode of awareness.* When writing your Haiku, express your feelings with words that describe your sensations. For example, notice in the above two poems words like red, heat, tight, and hollowness.

Dwelling Within Versus Detachment

For a moment, let's further explore what it means to *dwell within* a felt experience, since this is not a commonly understood notion. Before our allowing awareness can unravel our patterns of meaning, we have to first be *dwelling within* our felt experience. *Dwelling within* means feeling the experience as it is without assigning our own meanings to it. It's about becoming present to the experience and being able to describe what we are being present to. Once we can do this, we literally begin unraveling our habitual way of relating to the experience. Until we're able to do this, we have *not* been *allowing* but have been *controlling, manipulating or judging* our experience.

Don't confuse this concept of "allowing" with "detachment," the latter being a term used in many spiritual practices to describe greater freedom from selfish or ego-centered concerns. In the process of Deep Change that we're exploring here, we do *not* want to escape or push the experience into the background, as we'd do with detachment; rather, we want to *feel its living presence* within us—and this is a process of *acceptance.* With detachment, awareness fades; as a result, there can be no release from the tensions of attributing meanings. Acceptance allows us to step into the experience, to familiarize ourselves with it and work with it; detachment is a process of moving back into a safe, witnessing place, a position of non-involvement.

Our sense of who we are is unraveled layer by layer, aided by familiarizing ourselves with our experiences of ourselves and the world, not by detaching or distancing ourselves from them. The *allowing awareness* is a wondrous gift whose power is not widely recognized. In an allowing mode, we can be freed from our habitual entanglement with patterns of meaning. This can be a difficult and painful process because along with the freedom to open up to new possibilities we may very well have to abandon what has been familiar and safe for us, without knowing exactly where we are going next.

Grief and Fear

During the journey into the depths of your being, you may encounter aspects of yourself that seem to threaten your beliefs about who you are, as was the case with the man who considered himself selfless and generous, earlier in this chapter. No doubt we all possess aspects of ourselves that we judge as ugly or bad or in some other way unacceptable. Ultimately, through the material discussed in this book, you'll be able to begin the process of unraveling these perspectives and freeing yourself of the hold they might have on you.

Along with your letting go of parts of yourself, you may feel great sadness. At first this may seem like a contradiction; after all, aren't you seeking to be freed of these parts of yourself? But such is the course of this journey. Allow these feelings of sadness to move through you. You may, as you encounter your sadness, fear that it will last forever, or that you will be unable to carry on in your everyday life if you let yourself fully experience your sadness. It may be that your sadness will last for some time, but not forever. On rare occasions, people do take time out from their usual responsibilities to allow a period of grieving. This grief and sadness often comes in waves and if you let the waves move freely through you, they will soon subside, allowing you to comfortably continue your daily activities. Soon the dark unknown of these feelings of sadness or grief give way to a fuller, richer experience of your life and greater freedom to be who you truly are.

It would be nice at times like this to live in a world where feelings of deep sadness were not treated much differently from any other human expression, such as laughter or joy. What a luxury it would be to have everyone around us be completely comfortable with the expression of the full continuum of human emotions, recognizing that well-being, authenticity, and creativity can only come about by trusting in the fluid recognition of the human experience. The fuller awareness of our depths brings light into areas of ourselves that have been dark and lost.

Rainer Maria Rilke, the sage poet, advises us on how we might best approach the discovery of ourselves, that surely there are terrors but recognizing them for what they are can only be to our benefit. He says: "Perhaps all the dragons of our lives are princesses who are only waiting to see us once beautiful and brave. Perhaps everything terrible is in its deepest being something helpless that wants to be helped."

In one of the adventures in the *Narnia Chronicles* by C.S. Lewis, a very spoiled and unhappy boy named Eustace is turned into a dragon after he greedily pockets jewels he had stumbled upon in a cave. After suffering this condition for some time, the wise lion Aslan appears to Eustace and brings him to a large spring-fed well. Aslan instructs Eustace that he must take off his "clothes" (his dragon identity) before he can enter the healing waters. Eustace tries to do so but finds that while he can shed his dragon skin, like a snake there is always another layer beneath every skin he sheds.

After several of the boy's attempts to rid himself of his dragon skin, Aslan takes over and helps him by clawing deeply into his skin and removing more layers. This is painful, but Eustace is finally freed of his dragon skin. Naked and vulnerable, he stands before Aslan, who then throws him into the well, where Eustace discovers himself as a boy again.

In this legend Aslan is fiercely unrelenting in stripping away Eustace's dragon skin, freeing the boy from what is not his true nature. I have often thought of this story as depicting the shift I call the Unraveling, since it, too, can feel unrelenting, painful, yet also merciful. It is a reminder that throughout the process of Deep Change, we are being drawn into new depths where we join with dimensions that long for us and which has great gifts for us. But just as Eustace had to strip away his skin in order to receive the healing waters of the well, we cannot be delivered into our true self still garbed in our current "clothing."

Body as Crucible

Another image that comes to mind in contemplating the Unraveling is the *chrysalis*, in which the lowly caterpillar finds itself transformed into a beautiful butterfly. Truly, in the Unraveling, we sacrifice our current form for another. Like the caterpillar entering the chrysalis stage, we surrender portions of ourselves, recognizing the gravity as well as the promise of what we are doing. Along the way, it can be difficult to keep faith, and thus hold our course.

What we need to unravel will vary in degree and intensity with each individual. Sometimes the Unraveling may continue for several years, and we do not realize it until we find ourselves already entering the Stilling, which is Shift 4. Nor does the Unraveling always involve daily struggles or sufferings. You may notice that you move back and forth between Shifts 2 and 3 for a time. So don't be overly concerned about exactly what shift you are currently experiencing. Your journey is rarely along a straight line. What is important is that you understand the overall movements of letting go in each shift, the relationship between the shifts and what can support you in each shift. Sometimes in the Unraveling, we temporarily surface from our own individual depths, and find that we then move again through Shift 2, rediscovering and reentering our opening.

While this book is intended as a guide into an unknown and perhaps even mysterious territory, each person's journey of Deep Change is unique. Nothing I could say would fully prepare you for the uniqueness of your own longings or the depths from which the pull of those longings might originate. What you will be challenged to let go of, and what you need to unravel, will be dependent in large part on the depth you will enter in yourself if you're to join with the corresponding depth beckoning to you. You will, in any case, discover as you go along, the path to your own further individualization and refinement of your essential nature.

What we choose to fight is so tiny!
What fights with us is so great.
If only we would let ourselves be dominated
as things do by some immense storm,
we would become strong too, and not need
names.

When we win it's with small things
and the triumph itself makes us small.
What is extraordinary and eternal
does not want to be bent by us...

This is how one grows: by being defeated,
decisively
by constantly greater beings.
-Rainer Maria Rilke

Footholds

- Strengthening your *allowing awareness* is the single most important way you can encourage and support yourself in the portion of the journey we have come to know as the Unraveling.

- Review the footholds in the last chapter.

- Practice the art of *Inner Haiku.*

- Remember to use your breath to gently surround challenging inner experiences, not *in order* to relieve your present discomfort but to simply support your allowing awareness.

- Remember your longing.

- Along the way, see if you can notice a pull on you, something like gravity, a downward pull or pressure whose flow seems to move deeper inward. Let yourself give into it, if only for a few seconds. Notice where it pulls you in your being-body. Let yourself dwell there for a little while, just noticing and describing what you experience.

- Seek other people, whether friends or professionals who you can talk with about your experiences in the Unraveling. Find people who will support the development of your allowing awareness, people who will listen to you deeply, *without* trying to fix or analyze you.

- Be patient and gentle with yourself.

- Remember that what is being unraveled is only what is no longer useful or real to you. You may experience a great sense of loss and grief as this unraveling progresses. Let these feelings move through you and trust that these processes are indeed merciful.

I said to my soul, be still, and wait without hope
For hope would be hope for the wrong thing; wait without love
For love would be love of the wrong thing; yet is there faith
But the faith and the love and the hope are all in the waiting.
Wait without thought, for you are not ready for thought:
So the darkness shall be the light, and the stillness the dancing.
—T.S. Eliot, from
"The Four Quartets"

Shift 4: The Stilling

To experience the Stilling is to feel an extreme sense of emptiness, nothingness and desolation. One person described this shift as, "*an airless, vast vacuum where there is no movement. You have no self to go back to, nor future to anticipate. You're only suspended in and over an oppressive nothing, having no energy, nor the ability to hope.*" When you're in the midst of this shift you can feel absolutely isolated and lonely, as if experiencing something entirely unique to you, something that nobody else in the world has ever felt. Rest assured that right now, at this very moment, many other people are experiencing the Stilling. It is a far more common experience than you might suppose.

The Stilling is, to put it mildly, uncomfortable, and if we had a choice, most of us would never go there. Ironically, allowing yourself to be fully inside the Stilling when you're there is the only way through it. If you are willing to explore the feelings you are having, dwelling within them for even a relatively short period, you will find that the experience actually calls you to the future—your future. But don't confuse this with your own preconceived ideas of your future; rather, the future that beckons is truly unknown and new. The knowledge that there are potential benefits to be discovered in the Stilling won't necessarily lessen the discomfort you're experiencing but sometimes it can help to know there are other people going through what you are. The more you know about this strange experience, the easier it will be to deal with it, since this kind of knowledge can provide you with a roadmap for navigating this part of the journey.

Because our feelings in the Stilling are so strange many people fear sharing what they are going through. They keep to themselves, remaining reticent about what they are experiencing, even with their closest friends and life partners. In support groups I facilitate, when one person dares to express what she is feeling, many eyes around the room shine with mutual recognition, as if to say, "Yes, this is what I am feeling, too!" It is an enormous relief to be able to share this experience with those who know what you are talking about. For that reason it is a good idea to have at least one person in your life with whom you can comfortably discuss what you are going through. If you are fortunate enough to have a close friend like this, ask them to just listen as you *describe* your experience. Ask them not to help you analyze it or try to fix it. Be aware that not everyone can do this for you. Even when we are pretty open to a wide range of life experiences, we can feel threatened when a friend shares the experience of the Stilling. You definitely do not need others' fear at this time.

As with each of the seven shifts, the Stilling can be experienced to varying degrees of intensity and duration. It is also possible to experience this shift as peaceful and restful, and later in this chapter I will talk about this difference. However, it is much more common to enter the Stilling with a sense of isolation, feeling that some kind of ending or great loss is near at hand. Bernadette Roberts gives the following account of this stage in her book, *The Experience of No-Self*:

> *...my own condition was of being completely cut off (dissociated) from the known, the self, without any compensating factor to take the place of the emptiness so encountered. It meant a state of no feelings, no energies, no movements, no insights, no seeing, no relationships with anything—nothing but absolute emptiness everywhere you turn. The utter sterility of this state is all but humanly unendurable, especially for any length of time, and to bear the burden of complete unknowing is a weight that moment by moment threatened to crush me, although crush me without bringing death...*

Here in the Stilling, suspended in alien territory, a kind of nowhere place with nothing in sight, you may become like a stranger to yourself, and the world can seem a complete stranger to you.

You might have many questions while you're in the Stilling: What *can* help while I'm here? What is being asked of me? What happened to the pulling movement of Deep Change, which now seems to have vanished?

First, it is important to realize where the Stilling occurs in the movement from your familiar known self-and-world to a new and as yet unfamiliar possibility. At this apex of emptiness and disconnection you are at a threshold where you are on the verge of being released, to discover a new freedom. The truth is that you will probably not feel the promise of freedom right away. Think of yourself as stepping onto a new threshold taking you into a space where you've never before been. Remember that a threshold marks the boundary between two different spaces or, in this case, between one way of life and another.

While it may not feel like it, you are closest to the fulfillment of the longing that has been pulling you along throughout this bewildering adventure from the moment of your Unsettling. For now, in the Stilling, you may be in a lull but it can be helpful to remind yourself that this shift is not a static or stagnant place. Rather, consider it as being an integral part of an ongoing cycle, just as the rest between heartbeats is an integral and necessary part of that life-giving cycle. You are *suspended at the threshold,* which only means that you have yet to cross into your new possibility. For the moment, you have little or no evidence to convince you that the new possibilities are really there.

Suspended in this way, the threshold you have come to marks a momentary discontinuity between two ways of being—one you have known and which feels familiar to you, one that you have yet to discover. Knowing this, you are perhaps better able to understand why you are feeling as you do; hopefully, this realization will help you hold steady and stay open in this challenging territory. What are the alternatives once you've reached this auspicious place? They are to freeze up in fear or close down in despair, either of which will only prolong, or even stall your movement through this journey. For lack of understanding about the shifts of Deep Change, there may be a temptation to seek symptomatic relief, either in the form of medication or in behavior that masks the discomfort or pain. While escaping discomfort is a natural enough impulse in all our lives, doing so at this time can arrest any forward movement that the Stilling promises.

Letting Go Into the Unknown

In the Stilling, you are somewhat like a baby who has just left the womb. As you come out into the world outside mother's body, you are still holding your breath. You don't yet know that it is possible to fill your lungs and breathe on your own. You will learn this only when you let go with that first exhale and cry into the open air. That analogy describes the quality of the Stilling experience well. You have left the known self-and-world (the womb) but you have not yet fully let go into the unknown. You don't yet even know there is the possibility of taking that *next breath* into the future—much less stepping into the world where you will develop in ways you could not possibly know. How could it be otherwise? You cannot know or experience this new way of being until you have actually taken the next step and released yourself into it.

Sense of No Future

You may recall from reading the first chapter that I made a discovery about the sense of meaninglessness I was experiencing. When I let myself explore this meaninglessness, I saw that at the heart of it was the experience of not being able to imagine the next moment. This did not mean there was not going to be a next moment–though it certainly felt that way; rather, there was no way to *know* the reality of the next moment before it came. Standing between the unknown and the end of my familiar self-and-world, it was impossible for me to know what my future held, or if it held anything at all! This absence of a *known* posed the question, "What if there is *no* next moment whatsoever!"

What is it that makes the experience of such transitions possible? It's because most of us are unaware that we are anticipating each next moment through a lens of knowledge provided by our familiar way of being in the world. We are all dependent on this familiar lens and the patterns of meaning it provides. It gives us a predictable structure, a frame of reference and orientation with regard to our identity and our relationship to the world around us. At the Stilling we lose this lens, and with that loss comes the impression that we are without direction, purpose or meaning. Old patterns of personal identity seem to have fallen away. As one person put it,

"It was as though the very tapestry of my life and my world was unraveling. I no longer felt like the person I always felt like I was, and when I looked out into the world nothing seemed to be whole to me...just a very fragmented and disorienting time in my life."

An essential dimension of our awareness is our ability to imagine ourselves forward in time, that is, we envision ourselves going about our lives in the next moment. Our sense of who we are is dependent on the ability to assume that who we are and what we're about is continuous from moment to moment, moving from the present into the future. For most of us, this sense of continuity is wedded to our familiar pattern of meanings; it is an integral part of our self-and-world structure. And yet, we are usually no more conscious of this mechanism of projecting ourselves into the next moment than we are of our hearts continuing to beat within our chests.

To test how this mechanism works, think about waking up in the morning. You automatically begin picturing what you'll be doing that day, from getting dressed to fixing breakfast, to imagining where you will go, who you will be seeing, and how you'll interact with the people and your environment. You don't normally have to be conscious of this inner process since it all unfolds naturally, guiding you through the day from moment to moment. With Shift 4, however, the familiar patterns you project into the next moment seem to have vanished and you lose your ability to imagine yourself forward in time. No longer can you anticipate the next moment since your ability to do so is held in suspension at the threshold of the unknown. If you find this disturbing, bear in mind that no matter now it feels, it does not actually mean there is no future moment; it simply feels that way. There is a future but it will not be the same future you previously projected forward.

Fatigue and Loss of Will

During the shift we are calling the Stilling, you may experience fatigue and a loss of motivation and direction. This is not surprising when you realize that the pattern of self-identity that has dropped away was determining, in large part, how you experienced being in the world, how you were drawn into the world towards people, objects, goals and projects. Along with this loss of patterning about who you are in the world, you may experience a corresponding loss of personal will in all of your human dimensions—physical, emotional and intellectual. (It is a good idea to eliminate other possible causes for persistent fatigue.)

If you experience this loss of energy, it's important to remember that being tired and not having your desired level of energy is an enormous taboo in Western society, and is frequently branded as depression, laziness or indolence. It can help to remember that in the Stilling, it is possible to experience a kind of *zero point*, where you feel a total lack of interest and energy. If you can accept this and permit yourself to give into that level of fatigue, you will hasten your progress into the next shift.

George Kuhlewind, in his book *From Normal to Healthy,* describes the experience of the Stilling and how

important it is that we fully appreciate its promise in the movement towards true individual freedom and authenticity:

> *Today, he stands in the stillness, the windless absence, of all external impulses: in this protective situation, he could develop his own seeds of originality that do not follow from anything, since there is to be no more following. Understanding this state of affairs is called revolution. The revolution is unsuccessful if the lack of will is not recognized for what it is, or if it is experienced only intellectually, not with the whole mind and soul as a cosmic/human zero-point, making it possible for man to begin.*

People who follow a spiritual practice may experience this loss of connection as being abandoned by God or a Higher Power, or of simply losing touch with God and their own spiritual identity. Consider this statement from a participant in one of my workshops: "The nothingness around me was vacant of God." Accounts of the *dark night of the soul* experienced by saints and mystics articulate the experience of being utterly abandoned by one's God. Their familiar relation-ship to God had to end before a new kind of relation-ship became possible.

Being With the Stilling

Realize that this state of being suspended is involuntary and does not feel to be under our control. It is not as though we can just decide consciously to let go, for this would require an act of will and for the moment our will has been stilled; we seem to be helpless, and in terms of getting out of our predicament, we are. But there are ways to be with the Stilling that can make a significant difference in our experience of it and perhaps even shorten its duration.

Similar to the previous shifts, the best way through Shift 4 is to accept where you are and let yourself *be there,* just as you are. In order to be aware and open to your experience in the Stilling, it is important that you cease trying to change or judge where you are and begin to let yourself describe what you can notice.

Recall how in Shift 2 we are asked to accept our felt lack, tender spots and helplessness. Similarly, in Shift 3 we are asked to accept where we are and allow ourselves to be pulled down into our unknown personal depths, a descent that unravels layers of experiences, beliefs and self-identities. In Shift 4 we are asked to accept that we are not the self we were and allow ourselves to look out into what appears to be nothingness, or no-self. In the Stilling, our *allowing awareness* gives us what we need to face the challenge of observing and embracing the seeming absence of a next moment. There are some models from real life that can help explain how this works and why this *allowing,* or *letting go,* is ultimately more productive than *trying to take charge.*

When a painter talks about confronting a blank canvas, or a writer the blank page, they are describing what it is like to open to the unknown next moment out of which a new creation may emerge. To be sure, this encounter with the unknown can be humbling and challenging, even for the most practiced artisan. Just as with the artist or writer, this apparent nothingness demands your open and attentive presence and discernment. While it might not feel like it, the possibility of a new creation is close at hand. Author Anne Lamott describes this kind of moment in her own creative life as being similar to driving in dense fog, where you can only see a few inches in front of you and the whole picture is not in sight. People frequently describe Shift 4 as something like that fog. Here is one woman's description:

> *The world seems unreal and alien. Everything seems to be an illusion. I feel disconnected. I don't know who I am. I am dizzy, as if I'm constantly about to fall. I feel vaguely nauseated. Everything looks different. The angles of buildings stand out differently. There is more depth everywhere; depth I can fall into. I feel floaty and spacey. I feel I am in a fog; a fog settles in and around me. I am nowhere. I have nowhere solid to stand. There is nothing in me; no center, no anchor, no reference points, no identity.*

This sense of being in a fog provides a good image for comparing two contrasting ways to relate to the Stilling. In the first, we are resisting, judging, and trying to change our experience. Or perhaps we try to set it aside so that we can carry on in our familiar way, as before. In the second, we open ourselves to the Stilling and focus our attention on the quality of that experience. Here's the first way:

Imagine you are standing in front of your home and the fog comes rolling in, enveloping the trees, the house, and street, until everything takes on a shadowy presence. As you try to orient yourself in relation to this usually familiar scene, you become increasingly disoriented. Then the fog thickens and it becomes impossible to see much of anything, save perhaps your hand in front of your face. If you continue to try to get around in the fog, searching for familiar landmarks, you may feel increasingly lost, helpless and insecure, or at least less than confident in your ability to get around.

Now let's turn to the second part of our analogy, that is, being open to noticing the nature and quality of the experience of being in the fog. Let's say you commit your efforts to just experiencing this fog. You could turn your full attention to the qualities of the fog, how it feels on your skin, how it veils the landscape, its temperature, denseness, even perhaps its smell. In this second scenario you would stop trying locate the objects that you know the fog is hiding. You would instead be paying attention to the *fogness,* as it were, that envelopes you in the here and now.

In our first example, notice the tension of the experience, coming from your efforts to get *through* the fog, to manage in spite of it. In the second example, you can be more relaxed, and even enjoy the sensations of that moment as you stand in the fog with total acceptance, allowing yourself to just *be present with it.*

But what, you may ask, does all this have to do with how we experience the Stilling in our lives? Following our first example you'd be experiencing the Stilling as *the absence of what was familiar and meaningful* to you. Where there was once meaning and identity and purpose and energy, there is now seemingly nothing. But is this truly nothing or simply the apparent absence of the familiar, or of what once gave your life meaning? You are attached to the shadow of what and who you thought you were and how you should or did feel in the world, and you are desperately trying to return to "normal."

In the second mode, where you allow yourself to simply be in the present just as things are, without trying to change them or get around them, you make a significant shift. Your attention is no longer on what once gave you meaning and purpose and energy but on the present, where it appears that only the fog exists. Instead of focusing on what you are *not,* you become increasingly aware of *what is present* for you. You need to do nothing but let it be as it is.

Most of us experience the Stilling primarily from the first mode—trying to get around it, do away with it, get things to go back to "normal"—at least initially; therefore, even though we feel at the end of our known self, we are still attached to what was true and real for us in the past. We cling to what *once was* rather than allowing ourselves to be with *what is.* We have yet to open to the unknown, and are still holding onto a bare thread of our previously familiar patterns of meaning. I mentioned earlier that some people experience the Stilling as restful and peaceful. I believe this can occur when a person is being with the Stilling in the allowing mode, accepting and open to it.

Entanglements

Make no mistake, allowing yourself to be with the Stilling in an open and attentive way can truly test your mettle. One of the potential obstacles is any memories you might have of previous experiences in uncertain situations. These memories might intensify powerful feelings associated with being vulnerable, looming up in such a way that you believe you will be overwhelmed by you know not what. Experiences such as this can certainly deter you from holding steady in an open way as you step onto the threshold of this shift. If you have not already done so, consider what your associations with being in uncertain situations might be. Your awareness of them will make it less likely that you will feel threatened by them, and you will be more able to simply notice them for what they are—outdated early warning systems. The following story helps to illustrate how this works in real life.

Ellen, a woman I saw in my psychotherapy practice, would periodically find herself in the Stilling, which she described as "a place of banishment, a vast and desolate emptiness" that posed an impending sense of doom for her. She realized that her way of surviving was a kind of internal scrambling of her feelings that, in turn, motivated her to work very hard at a frenzied pace and with an all-consuming focus. This mode—the frenzied pace and sharp focus—allowed her to escape her uncomfortable feelings while also serving her well in achieving a high level of financial security and professional status as a successful attorney. However, there eventually came a day when her career was no longer satisfying to her. She now felt a longing for something more, a yearning for real connections with others, for a sense of belonging and intimacy. Whenever she experienced the Stilling, in which her scrambling way of life was also stilled, she became overwhelmed with a sense of isolation and impending doom. And so the cycle would start all over again for her as she used her scrambling lifestyle to shield herself from these dark, formidable feelings.

Ellen experienced the Stilling as a deep form of rejection, of being cast out from a place of warmth and belonging, whereupon she felt that her survival was literally at stake. She'd move into the Stilling, feel overwhelmed for some time, and then experience temporary relief through indulging herself with external distractions. As time passed, this pattern was becoming increasingly ineffective. For example, she would launch into a long and demanding legal trial that would require all of her mental, emotional and physical resources. Then, at the end of the trial, she'd find the Stilling waiting for her once again, opening before her like a barren and lonely abyss.

Through repeated visits to the Stilling, Ellen became *aware* of certain meanings she associated with it: banishment, threatened annihilation and hopelessness. By allowing herself to openly be with the feelings that came up for her in the Stilling, she soon saw that they were associated with experiences from the past. She was then able to shift her focus and *be with* the Stilling on its own terms. One day she reported that she had turned a corner. She felt a still emptiness all around her but it was a different kind of emptiness than before. She said that nothing was engaging her or pulling her out into the frenzied activity that had been a pattern for her in the past, but she knew it was okay. She was not reacting to this emptiness she was experiencing in the Stilling but was present with it in a kind of matter-of-fact way. She felt she was waiting for something but did not feel the sense of doom she once had. The doom was now a dim echo, like a pebble dropped into a deep well, which she heard and recognized but did not respond to it as she had done before. Here's how Ellen described it, in her own words:

> *I feel as though I am creeping over the top of some rocks, some kind of edge and am getting the view of a huge expanse, a vastness that awes me but does not draw me or engage me.*

Ellen's example shows us how the meanings we associate with the ending of our known self-and-world can distort our true perceptions of the Stilling, and that these meanings, which are offered to us in the Stilling, are what our familiar way of being is guarding against. We can begin to reap the true benefits offered in the Stilling only when we allow ourselves to cease whatever is our own equivalent of Ellen's non-stop scrambling mode.

Beyond Illusions of Specialness

In my mid-thirties I separated from my husband. At the time our son was four years old. This separation was a heart-wrenching yet necessary decision on my part. In the summer right after our separation, I rented a house on the Northern California Coast for a week's vacation with my son. In an effort to feel that I could still create some semblance of a family vacation, I invited relatives and friends with small children to join us for much of the week.

In the middle of the week there was a day for just the two of us, free of guests, and I felt relieved with the prospect of time alone with him. However, as evening approached, I sensed a dark, lurking emptiness in the periphery of my consciousness.

As I tucked my son into bed, his laughing, sparkling brown eyes and cheerful countenance made me feel like a fraud. A voice within reminded me, *I gave birth to him. I am his mother, teaching him about life, encouraging his love of life, acting as though life was meaningful and valuable. Yet here I am, worlds away from him, isolated in my encroaching emptiness and disconnection.*

I was very afraid. I said goodnight. He had no idea that we were eons apart.

I walked downstairs, frightened, nauseated and dizzy. I contemplated calling someone, wanting to reach out, to be saved from myself. I decided not to, but it helped somewhat to just know I had the option of contacting a friend. I frantically searched for my connection to myself and the world. I was confronted with my self-importance. I could see it everywhere I looked in myself—effort upon endless effort to *be something,* something significant and special. I felt shamed by this awareness, and humbled. I felt I was going to die. I was like a small boat adrift on the ocean, with all its moorings cut. My sense of nothingness overwhelmed me. I could not keep it at bay.

Then a small voice within said, *Stay with your experience, Susan, this is where you are and it is the only place you can be at this time.* I wondered if I dared to stay still with myself and let the nothingness overtake me. Somehow I knew it would only get worse if I tried to change my experience, but I felt so unreal and wayward that it was extremely challenging to sit tight.

With several transitions of Deep Change under my belt, I had a speck of faith, enough to let go and accept that I was nothing. I decided to take a bath, not in an effort to change how I felt but because I had been planning to take a bath anyway and I decided to just put one foot in front of the other and go ahead with my plans. I continued my routine in the midst of the sense of absolute meaninglessness and disconnection. Taking a bath seemed absurd. Everything seemed absurd. But I ceased trying to make sense or search for meaning and connection. I simply continued in the mist of the absurdity, surrendering to my nothingness. After a while, I began to experience something quite new—a kind of swift free-fall.

As I finished washing my hair in the tub I realized that my experience had shifted. I found myself patting my legs and thinking, *Here I am, I'm all right!* I was certainly not ecstatic but I was *found*—not where I had been before, but in a new place. This surprised me greatly. My panic was gone. I felt safe, tender and peaceful. I felt transparent, and was sure that if there'd been another person in the room they'd have been able to see right through me. I was substantial but my edges felt malleable. As the moments passed, I experienced a growing sense of gratitude, though childlike and tentative at first. I was okay. My dizziness was gone.

I slept well, deep, safe and cozy. The next morning my son and I went out to walk on the beach and visit the early morning tides. I was filled with a buoyant, subtle joy, a growing gratefulness for life. I felt curious and everything delighted me and filled me with a sense of awe. I felt no need to find meaning. My aliveness was enough. I realized that I was unique but so were each of the starfish that spotted the beach. I felt expanded but not self-important. I knew I was special because I was a part of life, no more, no less. And this was wonderful. This kind of specialness did not separate me nor isolate me as had my previous illusions of specialness and self-importance. Rather, I now felt joined with life, at one with it. This was a new beginning.

I had been journeying through Shifts 1, 2, and 3 for several months prior to that particular evening. When all distractions had ceased, my friends and family gone, my son asleep, I had found myself at the threshold of the Stilling. Bereft of a core part of my sense of self as wife and mother within a loving nuclear family, I had found myself drifting on a still and vast ocean, disconnected from what was familiar and reliable in my self and in my world. At the edge of an unknown future that had been beckoning me for quite some time, I felt my smallness and self-important attempts to be something more than I was, to be my own ground, my own creator. I felt a tremendous sense of humiliation as I saw everywhere how much energy I'd invested in trying to be something more than what I am. With the help of past experiences and the availability of understanding friends, I turned to face the nothingness, to allow its truth to enter me, and felt a letting go into thin air. But I was held. Up to that turning point I was attached to the remnant of what I was not, which was fueled by shame that echoed past accusations.

Caution in Times of Despair

Feelings such as shame, abandonment and fear of death, sometimes associated with experiencing the Stilling, need to be clearly understood for what they are. In the Stilling, some people entertain thoughts of suicide as a way to escape the despair they are feeling, or to regain some illusion of control. If you feel you are in danger of injuring yourself, it is imperative that you reach out and find someone you can talk to, ideally a person trained to help others through such crises.

In the Stilling, it is not uncommon to have thoughts about death or to vividly feel the possibility of our own deaths without these thoughts being suicidal. These thoughts and feelings are understandable since our familiar self is coming to an end and we have yet to experience the new possibilities on the other side of the threshold where we step into a deeper experience of our self.

One person described his experience in the Stilling as *waiting without hope.* This is what is required at the threshold of the Stilling, to wait openly, holding steady, without any sense of anything coming, but to nonetheless breathe and open into your stilled and waiting state of presence. Here are some of the ways you can find support through this period:

Footholds

First, remember that you are not alone. Find a person or a group you can talk to about your experience.

Second, understand that in the Stilling you are nearest to what is dearest to you, yet you may feel cut off from life and meaning as you've previously known them. Keep this truth in mind throughout the Stilling experience. This knowledge can give you the faith that it's okay to surrender to your present experience.

Third, describe your experience to another person or by writing in your private journal.

Fourth, become familiar with the meanings you associate with the "unknowns" you encounter in the Stilling.

These four techniques will aid you in staying with your experience rather than being tricked by these fears into an immobilizing tension.

An elegant poem by David Wagoner describes the kind of attention we need to develop at this threshold. The poem, titled *Lost,* is the answer a Native American elder may give to a young person asking, "What do you do when you're lost in the woods?"

Stand still. The trees ahead and bushes beside you
Are not lost. Wherever you are is called Here,
And you must treat it as a powerful stranger,
Must ask permission to know it and be known.
The forest breathes. Listen. It answers,
I have made this place around you,
If you leave it you may come back again, saying
Here.
No two trees are the same to Raven.
No two branches are the same to Wren.
If what a tree or a bush does is lost on you,
You are surely lost. Stand still. The forest knows
Where you are. You must let it find you.
— *"Traveling Light," Collected Poems*

If you can surrender to the Stilling, if you can let yourself internally *stand still,* to breathe into this place of no past nor future, then you can begin to look around and pay attention to what this place is like. If your intention is to allow things to be as they are, to be aware, open and receptive, then you will be able to inhabit this place; it will become familiar to you, a place you can comfortably revisit in the future. It may be difficult right now to imagine why you might want to revisit this place but this answer will become clear by the time you have completed this shift and moved on to the next.

As Wagoner's poem suggests, in this state of standing still, "noticing and open," you will be *found by something larger and other than you.* It is not up to you to try to find your way out of where you are, but to be still and receptively wait. It may be that in this receptive waiting, a deeper and silent unraveling is occurring, and the final strand will let you go according to a timing that is not yet yours to know or control.

A threshold is not a simple boundary; it is a frontier that divides two different territories, rhythms, and atmospheres.

— John O'Donohue, "To Bless the Space Between Us"

Shift 5: The Releasing

You are suspended at the threshold of stillness, a place where you can see no future, no next moment. You are not the self you thought you were. You see nothing on the horizon. You do not even see a horizon! The world has rolled away from you. In other words, at the Stilling our familiar self-and-world has unraveled and we are exposed to the unknown next moment, often to such an extent that it can feel like there is no next anything! However, we are not yet *free* of our familiar self-and-world; it is more like we are *suspended* between that which was familiar and a new way of being. There is still some kind of tension as though we were holding our breath.

In the Releasing, when we open receptively to the unknown around us, we experience a deeper sense of surrender, perhaps even a feeling of submission. In a gesture of pure faith, you let go. This is the nature of Shift 5, the Releasing. In the next moment you open to the possibility that perhaps you are nothing, or that nothing exists. It is not that you feel these changes as discreet experiences that you can name. If you were fully cognizant of what is happening during this shift, it's likely that you'd see what you are experiencing as a courageous opening. It can happen so subtly and quickly that you barely notice it or the part you play in it. Were it somehow to be replayed to you in slow motion, you might see yourself looking into the *nothingness* yet staying open to it, letting yourself fall into this nothingness, sliding into a place of no meaning, no self, no next moment. You would see that you have willingly surrendered your self and your life into the possibility of *not being*.

It's important to note that what you are experiencing is not resignation or despair. It is in fact a gesture of faith, not faith in any *thing* or any *one* or any *idea* or *belief*. Nor is it a withdrawal or turning away from life; rather, it is a willingness to pioneer a truly unknown territory, without any sense whatsoever that there will be any territory to experience. It is a willingness to let yourself go into an experience of *being nothing*.

As you step over the threshold into this unknown territory you may experience yourself poised at the edge of the known world while all around you, in every direction, you perceive an abyss. You cannot return to the safer ground of your familiar identity because that identity has unraveled and no longer offers you the support it once did. Given that this is so, you now stay open to the endless nothingness and, as you follow on, an opening appears. You now have stepped into the experience of the Releasing. And to your surprise you discover something quite different from the nothingness you expected. You enter a new way of being, one with surprising potential—the realization that there is no such thing as *nothingness,* only the challenging experience of *anticipating* nothingness.

Even more surprising is that in stepping into what you had believed was nothingness you have drawn upon resources within your own solitary depths. This achievement is yours alone, for you had nothing to hold onto or support you in moving into this place. There are vast and endless distances all around you—truly, you have faced the abyss. Out of sheer faith you have allowed yourself to *free-fall* into you know not what. When people believed that the world was flat, they imagined explorers falling off the edge of the known world and tumbling into endless space. Like the ancient mariners who challenged that belief, you dared step beyond what was known and proven.

Looking back from this new vantage point, you may reflect that you had been focused on the experience of some kind of impending annihilation, convinced that you were going to fall into nothingness. But now, having lived on, you've discovered there really *is* a next moment after all! The threat of annihilation was only anticipated, but does not happen. Prior to stepping into this shift, you just could not imagine you'd survive. Your capacity to imagine was momentarily stilled, continuing to be a bit entangled with the awareness that you were not who you thought you were. As your allowing awareness *turned receptively toward being nothing,* you opened to the next moment through no structure or knowing, yet you were radically receptive, nakedly open to the world you were then released into. Having moved into the Releasing you are suddenly affirmed in your existence, belonging to a new world of meaning and connection and possibilities. Your awareness of the Releasing can be sudden or more gradual, as it slowly dawns on you that you have changed and the world you now experience is different.

Here in the Releasing—what some might call *a point of radical discontinuity*—you are freed into an awareness where old ways of being and perceiving are wiped clean. As remarkable as this shift might be, it need not be jarring or disconcerting. In my account of my experience on the North Coast (in Shift 4) I accepted that I was nothing. Then, as I was bathing, I opened my eyes and found that I was in a new place. No fireworks, no ecstasy, just a very real sense of being held, of being alive and affirmed in my aliveness, transparent and vulnerable while utterly safe and wanted.

The Releasing is not under your control, at least not in the sense that you have your car under control when you drive or have control over a special skill you possess. However, you do allow yourself to become available to the Releasing when you open yourself to the possibility of being nothing. In effect, you *lay your burden down.* You finally experience the futility of trying to *be something* and let go of any efforts you might make towards that end. During the free fall into seeming nothingness that follows, you are released from your familiar world. Instead of acting from your known and familiar place, you step into being an individual who is real, whole, affirmed and open to the new and wondrous world now before you.

The Different Faces of Nothingness

What it means to *lay down your burden* is different for each of us and the meaning we assign to it may even change at different periods of our lives. In the account of my experiences in Shift 4, I described how I became excruciatingly aware of my need to be special and how hollow and empty those efforts suddenly seemed to me. That was the particular burden I was able to lay down. But this burden is not the one everyone carries, not by any means.

Frank was a young man who always felt he had to be more than he really was, regardless of his achievements or how others viewed him. That was his burden. His familiar way of being demanded that he always be more in control and more responsible for his life than was humanly realistic or even healthy. In the Stilling, where his swift descent through Shift 3 carried him, he experienced himself briefly as floating in what he called "a vacuous outer space kind of place." Then, in the Releasing, he experienced himself "being a zero, not a nothing, but coming down to zero." He felt an enormous relief because he was liberated from the burden of having to be more than he could be. In his known and familiar structure, where control and responsibility gave his life meaning and purpose, he had warded off the experience he encountered in the Releasing because he perceived it as a threat to his very survival. When he opened up and actually e*xperienced* being zero, he was surprised to find how peaceful and relaxed he became. For the first time that he could remember, he experienced his own individuality in a way of being that was outside his need to do the right thing and be in control. Here, with his burden lifted, he could *just be.*

During the Releasing, when the tension of what you are going through is most uncomfortable, it can help to remind yourself that there is something valuable and uplifting beyond losing the core beliefs that have, until then, seemed to give your life meaning and purpose. This simple knowledge alone can help you stay present with what may at first seem like personal annihilation.

From Being Something to Being

In the Releasing, we discover that the experience of Deep Change involves a movement from identifying with what we do, think and believe to a relatively greater awareness of our more essential selves. We could say that what unravels and stills in Shifts 3 and 4 are ideas and beliefs that were not essential to our truer natures, and in the Releasing we experience ourselves as more authentic, more real. We experience both a fresh freedom and a sense of coming home to our truer selves. It is challenging to describe the nature of this state of fresh freedom, but we can say that compared with our familiar self-and-world, we have gained a deeper capacity for experiencing—for be*ing*. In the Releasing we experience our self-and-world in a way that is unmediated through a familiar lens of perception, which opens us to a kind of awareness that is fresh, immediate and receptive.

What is most important is to realize that when we surrender to the possibility of being nothing we are released into the unknown next moment *freshly*—which is, by the way, the very famous and lauded *Now.* It can be very reassuring to remember that the moment before we are released into the truly *new*, the *present moment*, we may experience the greatest degree of not-knowing and possible nothingness.

Profound Individuation

To successfully negotiate the shift we call the Releasing, we must surrender, and we must move forward on faith. It is important to appreciate the gesture of faith by which you make this shift, and to realize that it involves a *commitment to deeper individuation.* In the Releasing, a radical maturation occurs. We step out of all that was holding us back and nakedly encounter whatever awaits us—even though we expect to step into nothingness.

In our western culture we associate personal growth with expansion, whether it be expanding into the Western Frontier or expanding into greater personal capacities. In Deep Change, however, we may feel we are getting smaller than who we have been or who we presently are. Who we may appear to be is disappearing or somehow diminishing. As a result, it can be difficult to believe that these shifts could possibly be leading to growth. And yet, you are, to be sure, pioneering a new frontier, and this exploration is essential if humankind is to have a future. Like the very first of our pioneering ancestors, we move forward not knowing the territory we are entering. Our journey into this new world of the human experience requires something very different from the muscle power and domination that allowed previous pioneers to claim victory. Where theirs was a paradigm of control, ours is a paradigm of surrender.

As different as it might be from the journeys of our pioneering ancestors, the tradition of individualism, self-determination and courage that motivated them also prepares us for this newest venture. We need to exercise different muscles of attention and apply self-discipline in new ways and towards different ends, yet our forebears have brought us to this point, teaching us to stand alone and think for ourselves even in the face of seemingly impossible odds. Today these skills make it possible to enter this new dimension of individuation with the capacity for self-awareness that our safe passage requires.

Understanding that Deep Change calls us into greater and more complete adulthood is important because the journey we are describing here stands many of our most familiar ideals of adulthood on their heads. For example, the cultural values of adulthood that we presently hold as incontrovertible include invincibility, knowing the right answers, being in control and in charge of our lives, and not being easily affected by the events around us. In contrast, Deep Change demands that we be vulnerable and open, with a willingness to not have answers, to knowingly yield to forces greater than our self.

We need a new vocabulary for this next stage of maturity. In forging that new vocabulary, we can better understand what is required of us, what will help and what will not support the Releasing. We need a way of talking about the Releasing that encourages us to yield to the unknown, not to resist it as a failure but to better grasp what it means to surrender to a deeper truth. Don't confuse this kind of surrender with collapsing into infantile helplessness. It's very different! However, the process does call for a certain kind of vulnerability, one that allows us to receive what is coming in while standing in our integrity. It requires a well-developed discipline of emotions, tremendous self-compassion, and an unswerving loyalty to the process to bring our allowing awareness into whatever experience is before us.

This next phase of becoming more authentic requires that we hold our own individual truth out, even as we forge into the unknown, beyond our familiar structure, without grasping for meanings or understandings or even calling out to be rescued. Consensual reality tends to look upon surrender as handing over our lives to a particular group of individuals who hold a specific religious, spiritual, political, scientific, technological, social or other set of values and beliefs.

Deep Change asks of us a much deeper act of surrender.

Small Spontaneous Gestures Can Make All the Difference in the World

It is all too easy to miss the moment when we make that faithful gesture of surrender—Releasing into the unknown. It can be so small, such a tiny opening, as though the force pulling us into its wondrous new depths is so close to us, just waiting for us to make that yielding gesture, and then, SWISH, we find ourselves in a new reality, experiencing a very different world. It is as though this force does not need much of an opening from us, just a crack. Perhaps it is no more than our little pinkie waving bravely and nakedly in the unknown air. This can be enough to bring us into these greater depths of being.

Keeping this in mind, it can be helpful to reflect on past times when you suddenly did something that was different than what you thought you would or could do. For example, you may recall that in my personal account in the Introduction of this book, I was lying on my couch that summer eve, and thought I would just continue lying there. Everything was so pointless. Why bother? But soon after having the awareness concerning the absence of a next moment, I found myself taking a walk. Something about going ahead in spite of the meaninglessness I perceived made an opening for what I then experienced as I stepped out into the evening air.

One woman reported being right up against the experience of being suspended in a vacuous void. She realized there was no way out. In spite of what she was experiencing, she went to her club to swim. Part way through swimming her laps she realized that a profound shift had occurred. She was now in a world of meaning and she experienced an exhilarating freedom.

Another woman, who lived alone, reported a very simple change that occurred when she went home from work earlier than usual. It was her habit to go shopping, go to a cafe, and then fill her time in some way in order to avoid the empty, lonely time before dinner. On this occasion she went directly home and as she turned towards this unscheduled open time for herself she experienced the Releasing.

Similarly, our friend Frank, who we talked about previously, had been struggling with growing panic and the impression that his life no longer made sense. He was increasingly unable to feel secure or to "get back in the saddle," as he described it. Then, at work, he was unexpectedly given time off. He was working near the ocean at the time. In this open time in the presence of the vast space of the ocean, he felt something give way, casting him into a free fall, deep into a peaceful and warm world where he felt a fresh freedom and deep belonging.

We can learn from these serendipitous experiences when we unexpectedly step into the unknown in some small, perhaps insignificant way. At such times, being out in nature can help move our process along because the beauty and spontaneity of the natural world can pull our allowing awareness into the next moment of the unknown without any effort or even awareness of that pull. Most of us trust and enjoy the beauty of nature. This trusting enjoyment can help us relax and experience at least some moments of letting go, which may be, at the right time, all that is required for the potential that is drawing us into the unknown.

In the movie, *Contact,* Jodie Foster is traveling in a wormhole, zooming through new dimensions of outer space. She comes to a stopping point, ending her downward movement. As she reaches for a cracker box token that her beloved had given her for safety (it is floating in front of her in the absence of gravity), she spies an opening in her space conveyance—a new world, the planets of Vega. She repeats over and over, "*so beautiful, so beautiful, a celestial event, they should have sent a poet, no words, no words, I had no idea, no idea.*"

Before being released into a way of being that is free from our familiar structure, we can have *no idea* of what we are entering because our capacity for getting ideas is perpetuated from within our familiar structure of self-and-world. In the Releasing, freed from what had been habitual and known, we find that we exist as a singular, real and affirmed being. At the same time, as we'll see in the next shift, the Spreading, our new way of being has a wondrous ability to experience the world in unimagined and surprising ways, and to also join more intimately with this new kind of world.

The Swan

This clumsy living that moves lumbering
as if in ropes through what is not done,
reminds us of the awkward way the swan walks.

And to die, which is the letting go
of the ground we stand on and cling to every day,
is like the swan, when he nervously lets himself down
into the water, which receives him gaily
and which flows joyfully under
and after him, wave after wave,
while the swan, unmoving and marvelously calm,
is pleased to be carried, each moment more fully grown,
more like a king, further and further on.

— Rainer Maria Rilke, *Selected Poetry*

I greet you from
the other side
of sorrow and despair
with a love so vast
and shattered,
it will meet you
everywhere.

—Leonard Cohen

Shift 6: The Spreading

In the Spreading, you are freed from your familiar ways of seeing and being. You experience the world freshly, immediately and naively. The truly new is now breaking through and discoveries await you that can be very surprising.

You'll recall in the Releasing that you found you did not disappear: on the contrary, you experienced yourself as being more essentially real and whole. Now in the Spreading, it is more real and more affirmed than ever. At the same time, in Shift 6, you experience yourself having the astonishing and wondrous capacity to Spread, that is, to unite instantaneously and unquestioningly with the world that has opened to you. In this Spreading you join more closely with the world, with the people around you, and with the relationships you have with everything around you. You are delivered into a deeper and fuller sense of connection, meaning and sense of belonging.

Herein lies the hidden promise of Deep Change. The magic of Deep Change hinges on our nothing less than miraculous capacity to spread our awareness into a new, larger and welcoming breadth in the world.

In the pages that follow you'll find stories that not only elucidate the Spreading but provide a picture of how the previous shifts work together synergistically, supporting the process of Deep Change that brings us to the Spreading and beyond.

Deep Calls Unto Deep

Through the first five shifts of Deep Change—the Unsettling, the Opening, the Unraveling, the Stilling and the Releasing—you have the experience of being beckoned into a deeper, more authentic dimension of your individual self. In the Spreading you meet and are received by that which has beckoned you. We could say that your freed awareness is the magical key that unlocks an entry taking you into a deeper dimension in the world. When your freed awareness meets with this deeper dimension, a new and larger *breadth* opens to you. Your awareness spreads, joining with this larger breadth. In Deep Change you are drawn into the deeper dimension, which is mercifully *unraveling* you into your more essential self, where a much larger world is unveiled to you.

Let's look for a moment at what we mean by *breadth* since this is an important aspect of Spreading. When we think of breadth, a sense of volume, or amplitude, comes to mind. Breadth evokes the idea of expansion into a space, a spreading out in multiple directions and dimensions. Why is the nature of breadth important for us to understand? Because it is central to how we grow beyond our familiar self-and-world structure.

Webster's College Dictionary defines *breadth* as "freedom from narrowness." One of the developments people describe in the Spreading is that their expansion into a larger dimension of the world gives them a greater ability to simultaneously see things, ideas, situations and people from multiple perspectives. They see many more possibilities than they previously saw. They feel more flexible and creative. (We will discuss these effects of Deep Change further in the next chapter, the Holding.)

During the process of Deep Change you are being drawn into a greater depth in yourself by a corresponding depth that exists in the world and whose existence you were previously unable to even imagine. Even so, you have been longing for the gifts of this new world just as this world has been longing for you. This reciprocity is, in essence, the "deep calling unto the deep."

When you let go and allow yourself to enter the unknown of the Releasing, you find that you spontaneously spread from that new anonymous depth into greater breadth in the world. And along with expanding into the larger breadth, you come into a more intimate relationship with a larger dimension of the world. You do not merge with this larger breadth so that you disappear; rather, the larger breadth comes into expression through your individual essence. What you had once experienced as being outside you, as separate and disconnected from you, even unrelated to you in any way, you now experience as near and dear. This is how we grow and transcend ourselves in Deep Change.

The Spreading clearly brings us profound and often mysterious experiences, as the anecdote in the section below will reveal. A closer look at this phenomenon will give us a better understanding of what is occurring and how we can support its fulfillment.

Spreading Is Not Projecting

You'll find the key to understanding the action of the Spreading by exploring the difference between "projecting" and "spreading." Projecting our awareness into the next moment is what most of us do most of the time. Think about the way a movie projector works. It projects light through images printed on a film and with the help of a lens casts enlargements of the images on the screen. Similarly, from within our own perceptual minds we accumulate stories, pictures, feelings and beliefs about our self and the world. We then project these perceptions out to the world, filtered through our familiar *mental screen* or *perceptual lens.* Our perceptions act as filters, allowing us to see and experience the world, things, and other people, always colored by our own preconceptions, shaped in part by our previous experiences of our world.

When we are projecting in this way we are imposing our habitual "film" onto the world, although we are generally not aware of how we are doing this. For example, we have all had the experience of misinterpreting a friend's intentions because we have preconceptions about the meaning of his or her actions. That's a very common form of projection. Projection perpetuates our familiar experience of our self and the world.

In the Spreading, however, we experience a naive encounter with the world. Our awareness opens out to the world, unmediated by our familiar stories, projecttions and perceptions about the way things are. Unfiltered by our preconceptions (which have unraveled in prior shifts), our awareness meets the world more nakedly and freshly. Some people experience the Spreading as an unaccountable shift wherein they see the world as if for the first time, fresh and sparkling. They know it is the same world they were experiencing moments before, but they are seeing a very different dimension of that world, one that they had been unaware of prior to the Releasing.

The following account is one man's sudden and very intense experience of the Spreading as he was trekking in the Himalayas:

> *What actually happened was something absurdly simple and unspectacular: just for the moment I stopped thinking. Reason and imagination and all mental chatter died down. For once, words really failed me. I forgot my name, my humanness, my thingness and all that could be called me or mine. Past and future dropped away. It was as if I had been born that instant, brand new, mindless,*

innocent of all memories. There existed only the Now, that present moment and what was clearly given in it. To look was enough. And what I found was Khaki trouser legs terminating downwards in a pair of brown shoes, khaki sleeves terminating sideways in a pair of pink hands, and a khaki shirt front terminating upwards in—absolutely nothing whatever! Certainly not in a head.

It took me no time at all to notice that this nothing, this hole where a head should have been, was no ordinary vacancy, no mere nothing. On the contrary, it was very much occupied. It was a vast emptiness vastly filled, a nothing that found room for everything—room for grass, trees, shadowy distant hills, and far above them snow peaks like a row of angular clouds riding the blue sky. I had lost a head and gained a world.

It was all, quite literally, breathtaking. I seemed to stop breathing altogether, absorbed in the Given. Here it was, this superb scene, brightly shining in the clear air, mysteriously suspended in the void, and utterly free of "me"...lighter than air, clearer than glass, altogether released from myself... There arose no questions, no reference beyond the experience itself, but only peace and a quiet joy, and the sensation of having dropped an intolerable burden.

—Douglas Harding, *On Having No Head*

Harding's description of suddenly having no head was the way he experienced an absence of any barrier between himself and the world. Where he usually felt a boundary, a distinction between himself and the world, there was none, and his free awareness spread into the world before him with such immediacy that he experienced actually *being* the world: "I lost a head and gained a world." And while he felt utterly renewed, he experienced the world as also refreshed, bright and shining, "clearer than glass."

While Harding's account is unusual, and may be unfamiliar to most of us, it nevertheless remains a good illustration of how the Spreading is a *spontaneous* action of our free awareness. In other words, we don't *try to connect* with the world more deeply. We don't exert effort towards finding more meaning. The truly good news is that as we are freed from our projections, that is, our predeterminations of who we are and how and what the world is, our awareness effortlessly *spreads into and unites with the world* that has opened to us; we not only encounter the world freshly and naively, we join more deeply with it.

A New Kind of World

To grasp what is occurring in the Spreading we need to understand the general nature and different characteristics of the world we meet and spread into as we are freed of our projections. As we are released into the next moment, freshly and nakedly, we discover that the world is not one of separateness and distances but one in which everything is related and connected.

It's important here to remember that people experience the cycle of Deep Change with a widely varying range of intensity. For many of us, our journeys of Deep Change happen gradually, over time, and within the context of our everyday lives. We may experience particularly low points and particularly high peaks as we move through the shifts. But eventually we realize that we have changed in some profound way, yet we cannot say exactly when or how this has occurred. You'll find two accounts of this kind of gradual journey of Deep Change in the upcoming pages that may be close to what you have experienced firsthand.

There are also more intense and concentrated experiences of Deep Change, like the one you've just read, and this may be true for you, as well. The seven shifts remain the same, regardless of the range of intensity, but the more concentrated experiences can seem very unusual in relation to our ordinary sense of reality. Several descriptions of more intense experiences are included here because they help to illuminate the nature of the Spreading. You may see parallels in these anecdotes with what you might describe as "mystical" or "spiritual" experiences. They may feel very unfamiliar, strange or beyond your reach. But I encourage you to not dismiss those that feel foreign or even otherworldly, because they can bring to light important insights about what is occurring in the action of the Spreading.

For example, in some of the more intense experiences of the Spreading, men and women who described themselves as "ordinary people, not mystics or spiritual," have reported seeing vibrating light or visible movement of some kind in the spaces between things and people, joining them, surrounding them, and holding them. This light and movement is not physical in the usual sense, yet it can be seen and felt. It can even seem palpable.

For the majority of us, everyday experience tells us that the spaces between things are empty, but we may discover something quite beyond that in the Spreading. We discover that this "empty" space is not empty at all but is filled with vibrant movement; we find here a world that is not of distances or sequences but rather is a kind of fullness that is flush with pulsating and interconnected aliveness. Our awareness, freed of our familiar perceptions and ideas about how the world is, spreads through and joins this fullness. Our open awareness shoots throughout this world, flush with aliveness, uniting with it. And we feel a very real and immediate connection with the world.

What you will soon discover as you experience the Spreading is that this world does not conform to the same laws of space, time and causality that your familiar, everyday experience seems to support. Some people experiencing the Spreading say that they feel they are *everywhere at once.*

Julie, who we met in Chapter Four, the Unraveling, walked outside following the meditation retreat where she had experienced the Releasing. She described her experience of the Spreading in this way:

> *I was nowhere and everywhere. The world was literally shimmering, with moving light around*

> *everything, between everything, including myself. I was shimmering inside and out. I felt an at-oneness with all life around me. Everything was so related; the trees and mountains were the same as I was. They were over there across the view and yet they were the same as me, somehow. I felt so connected to them. This was true of the people around me as well—they were all shimmering with the same light that I had and that everybody else in the world shared.*

If you will recall, prior to the release, Julie was "stuck in a tight spot" and her world was flat, devoid of meaning, stark, empty and inhospitable. But after the Releasing, and as she entered the Spreading, her world became full and pulsating, "shimmering" with life, which included and connected her intimately with her world.

The man trekking in the Himalayas described his experience of suddenly *having no head.* He tells us that the vacancy which suddenly appeared where he usually felt the boundaries of himself as a separate entity "was no ordinary vacancy... On the contrary, it was very much occupied. It was a vast emptiness vastly filled, a nothing that had room for everything." We could say that he experienced himself being nowhere yet being everywhere at once. He experienced no separation between himself and the world. Released from the personal identity that separated him from the world, he spread into the world and joined with it so immediately that he experienced *being* the world before him, everywhere at once.

The following account of a woman in her mid-forties is another description of a relatively intense experience of the Spreading:

> *There was a time in my life when I suddenly lost all my energy. Nothing medical could be determined, but I simply could not extend myself beyond the moment without feeling nauseated, dizzy and in need of immediate sleep. One day while eating lunch on my deck, I was describing this experience to my husband and how it seemed I could only be right in the moment, or I would feel all of the uncomfortable symptoms. It felt like a limitation. But as I described my experience to him, I was gazing at the mountain across the valley. I started to feel, or to know, what I can only describe as* the shape of the mountain, *as though it was so familiar it seemed to be inside my own body. I felt a very intimate connection with the mountain–I knew from inside me the gesture of the mountain. I knew its shape from inside my experience. I started to cry. The air was infused with a palpable presence, with an aliveness that I could see and feel; it was vibrating. This palpable presence filled the spaces between things and it was holding the world. The only thing I could say is that it was love. My experience was very startling, while absolutely undeniable and tremendously comforting.*

We can see that as this woman was reined into the moment, into the *now*, and she could not move forward through her usual ways of being, her awareness was released freshly. It then spread into the world before her in an unmediated, naked mode. As her awareness spread into the full aliveness that pulsated in the spaces between her and the mountain, spaces that she ordinarily perceived as emptiness, she felt an immediate and intimate connection with the mountain. She knew it as herself.

The above anecdotes illustrate how the deeper dimension of the world that we encounter and spread into is filled with greater possibilities for real connections that were unavailable to us from our familiar self-and-world relationship. And this is true for us regardless of the relative intensity of our journey of Deep Change. In the Spreading, as we drop ways of being and relating that separate us from the world, we instantaneously join more freshly, immediately and therefore more intimately, with an expanded breadth of aliveness in the world. Our arrival brings us more meaningful connection and a sense of unquestioned belonging.

Two Stories of Deep Change

The following two accounts of Deep Change, while perhaps easier to relate to in the context of our everyday lives, are by no means any less potent and transformative than some of the more intense descriptions above.

Leah

Leah was in her mid-fifties when she began to lose interest in her high-powered job as a CEO in the fashion business. People surrounding her at work catered to her and worshipped her. "I was the queen," she reflects. One of her greatest gifts, for which she was most respected, was her sense of design and color in retail apparel. She traveled the world, drawing on creative inspiration from many different cultures. Leah's life was full of riches and creativity.

However, she started to feel a gnawing emptiness. Out of the blue, she took a horse trip, bought a horse and, shortly thereafter, a ranch in northern California. Then, as these enchanted stories often go, her current employment ended, and instead of seeking other employment, which was readily available to her, she moved to her ranch, bringing with her the stable hand that had cared for her horse in Southern California.

Here we feel the pull of a new longing in Leah's life. She had felt empty and wasn't sure what she wanted to do, but then she took the radical action of moving to an isolated valley up north to be closer to some of her family. She was *Unsettled.* Then, after she relocated, she began to experience a tremendous amount of sadness, grief, and desolation.

Once the excitement of the move and change wore off, once winter settled in to the narrow, rugged valley where I now lived, I became absolutely despondent. I felt a great sense of regret for having left the life I knew and had thrived in. I felt a tremendous sadness. I felt I had made an enormous mistake. I was no one here in this place of plants and animals and country people. They had no idea of who I was—or, had been!

One day, a new friend of Leah's suggested that it was okay if she allowed herself to just be with her sadness instead of trying to figure out what it meant or how to get rid of it. This was a very new concept for Leah. Somehow, she had always assumed that feelings like sadness were an enemy, but now something felt right about accepting it. As she let herself dwell within her sadness (the Opening), she began a descent into layers of grief and loss.

I let myself cry, to feel the enormous sense of loss, the emptiness, the sense that I had lost track of who I was. What was my value?

Also at about this time, I was gifted with a kind of waking dream, a very vivid image that had a profound impact on me. It was of a little girl in a tree house or playhouse of some sort, and she was very happy and focused on her little tea set. Unbeknownst to her, I was watching her and felt a strong affection for her. I knew she was a part of me in some way. Then the little girl looked out from the tree house, gazing, seeking something in the distance in front of her. From behind her, the sun was rising and as its rays shone around her head, an explosion of the most beautiful and delicate colors shot out all around her! They were an array of rainbow colors, vibrant and dazzling! All shades—so beautiful! The sun was shining through these colors, lighting them as though from the inside. But the little girl was not seeing these colors. They were behind her and she was looking outward—the other way. But I could see the colors. I loved them, they were almost too beautiful to behold, and they touched me deeply. I wept. I knew that these colors were telling me that something was coming, something I could not yet see nor imagine, but was very real, beautiful and promising, none the less.

This vision was a mystery to me but held great power. Somehow, it gave me the faith I needed to believe in the decisions I had made and persevere through the difficult times and feelings I was experiencing. It gave me the courage to wait and stay where I was, even though I felt very isolated and disconnected from life.

Leah first experienced the Stilling as very dry and desolate, but slowly she let herself enter the quietness of that place, becoming more comfortable with just being in her natural world and not rushing from one project to the next, as had been her habit. Periodically, the numinous would break through unexpectedly, and Leah would feel a deeper connection with the world around her.

In the midst of my sadness and loss and confusion, I had amazing moments of connection with nature—

with the pleasure of putting the chickens to bed, with the beauty of the lavender and the bees, and all those wondrous birds! I had moments of such an intimate connection with the life around me; they came out of the blue, surprising gifts that helped sustain me through the next wave of sorrow and emptiness. I had lost track of my childhood sense of awe, but it was now rekindled.

Leah was gradually able to note how the beauty and wonder around her was opening up to her as she became quieter and her familiar ways of coping were less accessible. Her awareness was progressively released from her habitual lens, and as she spread into her world more nakedly, stripped of her former identity, she began to experience a closer connection with nature, a relationship that was new and surprising for her. This rebirth of "wonderment" gave Leah hope.

In the meantime, Leah's ranch manager, her former stable hand from southern California, who lived on the ranch next to hers, had gotten married and now had a daughter. Leah developed a strong bond with his daughter and came to be called her grandmother. Again, this connection surprised and delighted Leah. This is how she described the growing bond with the girl:

I became her grandmother and she loved me as such. She daily bounded over to my house to play with me. This joy of having her in my life was so unexpected! Then one day, while water coloring at my house, as she carefully dipped her brush into

one of the many colors all lined up in glass bottles, the sun shot through the glasses from behind her, lighting them up, and I gasped. These were the colors from my vision some years ago!
The precious connection with this "granddaughter" had been foretold in that vision, and was even present in my connection to my first horse, which brought my granddaughter's father up to my ranch, although this little granddaughter was just a star in his eyes at that time. And my relationship with her is wondrous on its own right, but also, it has brought me into deeper community with others who love her.

Now, in addition to my intimate relationship with my granddaughter, I am finding myself entering into community with others in a way that is meaningful and nourishing to me, in ways that are very surprising to me! I am not the "Queen" as I was in my former life, but my riches are surpassingly more satisfying and my connections far more real and sustaining.

Before, in my former life, I never really knew if people were drawn to me because of my success or if they just really liked the real me. Now I know that they just like me, and that is an enormous difference! More simple and more real. I feel so grateful for the fullness of my life! It is the real connections that I feel that is the difference.

When we look at Leah's story, we need to see that her arrival–into deeper meaning and connection with herself and the world–occurred as her increasingly unencumbered awareness had the freedom to *spread* into the world that had been beckoning her. The promise of this new possible relationship with the world showed itself to Leah in the vision she had of the little girl and the wondrous colors. She didn't, at first, understand the meaning of the vision, but it served as a kind of beacon in the darkness, supporting her in times of great *lostness* and isolation, encouraging her to allow these difficult experiences.

Often in the journey of Deep Change, help or support arrive unexpectedly. We may miss its appearance if we are primarily fighting against our experience, for example, fighting against the Unraveling. But if we can be a bit more open and allowing, then it seems that we are sent signs, emissaries from the world that is calling us forward; we discover the presence of tiny lamps in the dark, guiding us along the right path even though things may feel bleak and devoid of meaning and connection.

Dawn

Dawn is a fabric artist. Through her own journey of Deep Change we see how her relationship with her art mediums opened into greater dimensionality, as did her relationship with the world.

When in her late fifties, Dawn had grown very lonely and very tired of how things were going in her life. She consciously started a journey of self-reflection, and soon became confronted with the falsehoods of core beliefs she had about her self and the world:

> *In short, I realized that I had felt a victim to others' judgments and rejections and that anger at the world had been my predominate experience. As I began to see the delusional nature of this story that I had created and sustained, I was thrown into a state of emptiness and despair. If this story is not true, then what is? Who am I? I may as well disappear.*

Dawn felt unsettled but she opened to her experience of emptiness and loneliness. She went through a time when she experienced layers of her old ways of being in the world simply being stripped away.

> *After my initial reaction of despair about each new truth subsided, I noticed that I felt a release in my body–it was very physical–like something was letting go. These physical sensations were very real and they helped me to trust a bit more in what I was going through. It was like something more was going on in me than just the dawning realization of terrible and shameful truths. There was some kind of new movement that was not in my head. It was not an idea. It was concrete–I felt it.*

Here, you might observe, Dawn is describing her experience of the Unraveling, in which she feels literally a loosening of habitual tensions that had maintained her familiar ways of being in the world. We can see that she was in touch with the descending pull of her longing, and although she was not fully conscious of this, it was a comfort for her to feel its movement.

Also guiding and supporting Dawn at this time was a recurring image in which she was suspended from a helicopter over a large body of water that was called "The Lake of Infinite Sorrows."

> *While I was terrified I would be dropped into this endless sorrow, I was curious about the image. It kind of oriented me, I guess. Helped me know where I was. Then after weeks and weeks of feeling the emptiness and great regret of how I had been living my life, I realized I had been lowered into the lake and was experiencing the great sadness and loss that my former anger had kept me from feeling.*
>
> *But then one day, in the image, I was lowered into a vast space below or underneath the lake. It was empty and I was alone, but as I sat there in this space, I noticed how beautiful the light was in it. How peaceful and calm it was, and that it was a relief to be alone in this space. I loved the lighting! It was soft and golden and yet very clear.*

Note how Dawn's image and its development vividly describes the movement from the Unraveling into the Stilling, Releasing and Spreading. Below her great and infinite sadness she is lowered into the vast and empty space of the Stilling. As she opened to her aloneness in this vastness, she felt at home and held in a golden softness.

Meanwhile, in her everyday life, Dawn started to notice other truths about her self, not just the falsehoods but characteristics and needs that were true for her. She became aware that she really wasn't enjoying contact with her fabric artist friends. She realized she didn't like the craft fair scene, and the friendships were too casual for her.

I became aware that I wanted deeper connections and that I was not interested in art that could be easily duplicated for sale purposes. I did not feel angry with this group, or critical of them. I just realized that I longed for and needed something different.

I decided to commit the time I would usually spend with them to staying in my studio. This wasn't always easy. Sometimes I would just look at fiber art magazines, or just rest on the floor, but I would be in my own studio. In time, a magical zone would open up or rather I would become immersed in it. I would focus on very specific areas of a piece of cloth I was working on, not trying to control the outcome of the whole piece, and wondrous things would happen (and still do)!

I would let go and sink in and begin to experience new relationships between the colors, the textures, the sticking. There is no time in this zone, the light is very good and nothing is in the way. It was thrilling yet also very calm and the air was clear like the space under the lake.

The rest of my life paralleled, in many ways, the new multiple relationships I discovered in my studio with my art. As old grudges left me, I felt greater compassion for people. For example, I ran into a former boyfriend with whom things had ended bitterly for us both. I felt friendly and warm towards him, but my smile and hello were greeted with a cold stare. In the recent past, this response would have got me on my self-righteous anger roll, but instead I suddenly had an image of him as a little boy who was not given what he emotionally needed. Instead of seeing him as mean or cruel, I saw his hurt and felt a flood of compassion towards him. This kind of dynamic occurred with many key people in my life who I had put in boxes to justify my anger.

Also, my senses seemed enlivened. Taking a walk was now a great joy. The cool air on my skin is perfect and the beauty around me often overtakes me—the flicker of a bird is so exciting!

I recently realized that I'm being pulled to move to a more urban area where there is more going on in the fiber arts world. I can accept that I'm not the earth mother I thought I should be in the 1970s. I don't want a big garden, I don't like hikes in the country, I don't like to can, etc. I want to be working on my art and going to museums and lectures and all of the things a large city offers. It feels so good to accept these truths about myself and they are not out of defensiveness or anger. They just are true and I feel so much more a part of the world, immersed into the world as I am with my art in my studio.

We can follow the different shifts in Dawn's story of Deep Change just as we did with Leah's. In her studio, as well as in all other areas of her life, Dawn's awareness *spread* into new depth in the world as her relationships to her art and to other people in her life were no longer frozen in the frame of her former way of being. She was able to connect with different dimensions of people and could hold a variety of perspectives simultaneously.

The development of Dawn's fabric art is a wonderful metaphor for what happens in the Spreading: once freed to do so, through the shifts, our awareness *spreads.* It moves throughout a wide variety of possible relationships in the dimension of our world that has been pulling us into the unknown. At last we join with and bring to light that which is truly new.

While the stories of Leah and Dawn describe more gradual experiences of Deep Change, they are nevertheless stories of real transformation. We can sense the numinous rising from the deeper dimensions that are breaking through. Leah and Dawn saw the vivid and enchanting images from the worlds that beckoned to them, ultimately sustaining them in their journeys of Deep Change. These more gradual experiences show us how, in our everyday lives, we are given the opportunity to digest and assimilate the experiences of the shifts according to our own rhythms and time, even as we are letting go of familiar ways of being and spreading into greater connection and belonging.

Contact at a Distance

The ability of our free awareness to spread allows us to experience the forces and connections that live in the *spaces between.* The Spreading allows us to experience what I call "contact-at-a-distance." This phenomenon can feel most mysterious to us since it goes against our familiar laws of space, time and causality. How is it that we can experience being "everywhere at once" or feel the presence and experience of another person? As your freed awareness spreads through the world you have entered, and even though you remain an individual entity, you can experience the living presence of another person or life form as if it were inside you. If not inside you, you can experience their presence across the apparent distance, often transcending the differences and spaces between you.

We see evidence of contact-at-a-distance in Julie's experience of the Spreading, described above. She came into intimate contact with the trees across the way, as well as with other people from whom she had felt so separate a short time before. The person reporting his surprising experience of the Himalayas was also describing contact-at-a-distance.

You have most likely experienced moments of contact-at-a-distance in your everyday life when suddenly something drops away and you perceive in a new light someone you have known for years; at this moment, it is as if you are seeing them for the first time. You may have a wave of compassion or affection for them, feeling their experience within yourself. We commonly call this "empathy" or "intuition." But do we really understand what allows this empathy to arise? We also commonly refer to this kind of experience as "open-heartedness," but how does this kind of openness allow us to feel another's experience?

What we drop or let go of in these everyday moments is some idea, a preconception about our self and the other person that has prevented us from clearly seeing and feeling them. We have been perceiving them through our projections, and when some significant part of our familiar lens has dropped away, our free awareness then spreads into the space between the other person's self and our own; we meet his or her experience as he or she feels it, rather than in terms of our usual assumptions and self-protecting filters or screens. Frequently at these times of clarity, we feel more meaningfully connected with that person.

Each of us deeply longs to be seen clearly and received for who we really are. Understanding the often invisible action of the Spreading points us in certain directions and toward certain practices that will enable us to more clearly see the way and allow us to enter the greater intimacy we so deeply desire.

As you spread into a new dimension of the world, what had been outside and separate is now experienced as very near, if not right inside you; at this point your contact with the world is intimate and real, often profoundly so.

You may remember my personal account in the introduction where I described how it was to step outside for a walk, not knowing if there would be any ground to hold me in that step. In that moment I discovered a new world, new because I was now experiencing it from a different depth of my awareness. Everything was shining and exquisitely vivid, rich with color and detail, filling my senses. And I felt I was participating intimately with all the beauty and aliveness of the world. Though I was standing on my front porch, I experienced the sounds of water across the street not as outside but as *inside* me. I experienced the sweetness of a little intimate conversation people across the way were having about the day's end, even though I couldn't hear the content of that conversation. My awareness was over there, experiencing the sweetness of their sharing. I felt touched and connected. The sense of emptiness and meaninglessness that had permeated my being just moments before was now replaced with a world of vitality and meaning to which I felt I unquestionably belonged. All that I experienced was brighter, richer, more alive and pulsating.

It is important to note that you do not remain in the pure state of the Spreading indefinitely. Our world, while deeply changed, eventually resettles into a more everyday reality, that is, what most of us refer to as "normal reality." And yet a new relationship between our self and a deeper dimension in the world has been forged.

Remember

Your spontaneous capacity to spread your awareness into the world as it becomes free from your known and familiar ways of being and perceiving, is the answer to your deepest yearnings for belonging in the world and, perhaps more important, for being welcomed by the world for being your true self.

The dynamics of the Releasing and Spreading reveal the truth that as we become more and more our essential individual nature, we also become more and more able to spread into and join with deeper dimensions in the world; it is here that we experience an increasing sense of connection and belonging, often beyond our wildest dreams.

It is important to grasp the phenomenon of the Spreading because this understanding will give us greater faith to dwell with our most vulnerable experiences. From the perspective of the Spreading, we can look back to the other shifts and see how the gifts of the Spreading became available to us as we allowed ourselves to dwell with some of our most threatening and challenging feelings: our flaws, our emptiness, our meaninglessness, our grief, our *lostness,* our anxiety, our sense of failure, helplessness, hopelessness, etc. In our Western culture, there is a great need to develop and sustain faith in what is most tender and vulnerable. And so, in understanding how our awareness spreads into new depths as it is freed from the known, we realize that it is essential to place our trust in the very subjective territories we have been taught to avoid all our lives.

...Flow down and down in always
widening rings of being.

—Rumi

The place you would fall becomes
in falling
the place you are held.
The great sea
and the still ship of your own
becoming…

—David Whyte, "Millennium"

Shift 7: The Holding

In this final shift, the Holding, the cycle of Deep Change draws to completion and we experience a sense of having arrived, of being *found and held* by a presence larger than, and other than, ourselves. We are now held by and within the larger dimension that has been beckoning us since the Unsettling, and we feel an unquestioned sense of belonging. Nor is this larger *other* neutral about our arrival. On the contrary, we are welcomed by it. It matters that we have arrived. We feel ourselves wholly received, discovering that who we are is exactly who is wanted.

Meister Eckhart says that we expand into our fullness when we are desired by an other. In that respect, we cannot find ourselves by ourselves. We need to be found by an other, one who desires us. In the Holding we experience being found by this other whose longing for us has beckoned throughout the process of Deep

Change. We do not unfold from solely within ourselves. The truly transformative growth of Deep Change involves a dynamic *relationship* between our individual self and the other—and this other is the larger dimension into which we have now spread and joined. This other is not simply a larger part of our self; it is truly *other than* our self. When we spread into it, we join intimately with it.

In the experience of being found we feel that we have come home, and yet, at the same time, the world we now inhabit seems new and fresh. The first five shifts of Deep Change, beginning with the Unsettling, involve a progressive letting go, a leaving of our familiar world. We could say that we began the process of Deep Change by being cast out of what was our homeland. Our known world unraveled and we experienced a loss of our familiar reference points; we became disoriented and even lost. We descended into inner regions that had once felt inhospitable and perhaps even threatening. We found ourselves suspended in the groundless province of the Stilling, possibly experiencing extreme estrangement from all that was familiar, in a vacuum starkly void of what had nourished us and given us a sense of connection to life. Opening to the possibility of nothingness, we find that we have been released into a fresh freedom, a real and affirmed individuality that has the capacity to spontaneously spread and join with a new and larger breadth in the world.

In the Holding, as we experience being found and welcomed by the other that has been beckoning us throughout this entire journey, we discover that we are, again, not only on solid ground but on new ground. We could say that where the Spreading is a kind of *soaring*, the Holding is a kind of *landing*. Even as we arrive at this new ground of the Holding we do not experience it as a foreign world in which we are strangers. Rather, we experience our arrival as a *homecoming* where we are not only embraced but even celebrated for being just who we are. This very personal and warm reception allows us to relax and begin orienting ourselves to this new world. In the Holding we begin to resettle, not where we had been, but in this new territory of a larger dimension in the world.

All the developmental stages that have been unfolding in our lives have involved openings into a vastly larger world, offering greater possibilities for exercising our own potential and for experiencing a greater range of relationships with people, things, nature, ideas, etc. Take as an example the earliest developmental stages of life: Prior to our birth, we are held within the watery world of the womb. When we are born, we enter a much larger world than we have thus far known, with space around us and between our self and others. This new open space, without the surrounding presence of the amniotic fluid and mother's protective womb, takes some getting use to. What helps a new baby acclimate safely in this new world is the love and warmth of his or her parents, family and friends. The infant is held close to the warm bodies of these loving and welcoming others, and even wrapped securely in blankets at first to give him or her time to relax and slowly stretch out into the new space according to a timing and rhythm that is gradual and comfortable. (We all know that suddenness, trauma and shock at this tender time can have harmful and limiting impacts on a human life.)

As the infant becomes secure in a welcoming and safe atmosphere, he or she discovers the loving faces of parents, in particular the mother's face—and particularly if she is breastfeeding. The relationship established with the welcoming faces and bodies of these others only became possible when the infant leaves the familiar world of the womb and thus enters a new and larger world. Similarly, when a child is weaned and joins the dinner table of the family, a larger world of possibilities opens. In addition to experiencing increased independence with each of these developmental stages, the child comes into new ways of relating with his or her family. Again, this development needs to be gradual so that the child can integrate each change in a way that is not a loss of connection and love, but rather an opening into a larger world into which the child is welcomed and enjoyed in the more complex context of the family.

Likewise in Shift 7, the Holding, our experience of being welcomed and wanted by the larger dimension that has beckoned us forth from our familiar world, provides a secure ground where we can get used to this new breadth and begin to exercise new capacities and ways of being that were made possible in Shift 6, the Spreading. The Holding reveals to us that in Deep Change, we do not spread indefinitely. Once released from our familiar world, we spread throughout a larger breadth in the world, uniting our individual awareness with this new dimension.

We are embodied beings and need ground and time to integrate the new gifts of the larger dimension we have joined. The Holding provides us with the opportunity to do this, to integrate the transforming experiences of the Spreading. Like a newborn in a new world, our eyes need to adjust to the new light; we need to gradually stretch our new muscles of awareness. We can look around and notice the characteristics of this new world and how it feels to us. In the Holding, the real treasures of our journey of Deep Change begin to be revealed to us.

The new freedom of the Releasing, the deeper connection of the Spreading and the unquestioned belonging of the Holding are all universal gifts of Deep Change; they provide the basis out of which other possibilities and our own capacities can emerge. We could say that the Holding is also a time for experimenting with these new possibilities and for mastering our new capabilities. When you first learn to walk as a child, an entire new world of possibilities opens to you, but at first you are awkward; your capacities expand as you explore these new possibilities, and with practice you realize the full potentials that they offer.

As you enter Shift 7, the Holding, you may discover abundant variations and ranges of intensity with regard to the ways you are transformed. You may experience some increase in your ability to perceive ideas, events, people and things from multiple perspectives at the same time. No longer limited to a singular way of relating to the world, you can more easily see things, events, ideas and people from more than one viewpoint. Recall in the

Spreading how awareness filled the new breadth that was opened, an experience that some people described as being "everywhere at once." That conscious awareness, thus spread, allowed us to perceive things from expanded viewpoints.

The increased access to a variety of perspectives in the Spreading allowed us to be more creative and effective problem solvers and to become more flexible collaborators. We found we were less interested in just being "right," in having the right answer or just making others agree with us. We found that we were more interested in hearing the truth of an other and more trusting of approaches in our work and play that support the deeper connection with the world experienced in the Spreading.

One man who experienced the cycle of Deep Change in his late fifties had been a divorce attorney for many years. He had the reputation of being a very aggressive lawyer in the divorce courts. As he arrived in a new relationship with himself and the world in the Holding, he gradually found himself more interested in facilitating mediation between the divorcing couples he represented, and less interested in litigation. He found he no longer had an appetite for the aggressiveness that had won him his reputation. He was now drawn to working in ways that encouraged people to listen and understand one another, as opposed to being pitted against each other. It's also meaningful to note that this man had not *decided,* in some conscious plan, to change his way of working. Rather, he found himself drawn towards a new way–even welcomed into–a way that supported the deeper connection with the world that he experienced in the Spreading.

In the Holding, it's as if we discover a new inner compass, one that points new directions and gives us a tool for orienting ourselves toward actions we might take in this new world. Yet we do not necessarily see the whole path or outcome of our actions in this world, at least not at first. We discover that this compass is sensitized or magnetized to the possibilities that will bring to light our new relationship with the larger breadth opening to us in this world. In the Spreading, our individual awareness, fresh and open, penetrated a deeper dimension in the world, and at the same time, we became infused with that same dimension. In the Holding, integration of this union proceeds as we create and manifest new ways of relating and doing things in our everyday lives, ways that make concrete and visible the transforming impact of the Spreading. I like to think of this dynamic as a dance of co-creation in which we partner with the larger dimension and bring the truly new into expression in our everyday lives.

In the story of the divorce attorney, he let himself be drawn to new ways of doing his work that were congruent with his newly unfolding relationship with the world. Gradually he realized that his law practice had radically changed in ways he had not consciously set out to effect but with which he was very pleased.

There are many different ways that people detect the trembling needle of their new compass. Several people have described this experience as a kind of "sparkling" or *inner effervescence* when in the presence of a choice or direction that is congruent with their new relationship with the world. Others have described the experience as a wave of warmth or of goose bumps, while some report just a clear knowing that a certain step or action is the way to go, again, without seeing exactly where they are going, nor how they will get there.

When Leah, whose story was in the last chapter, found herself in the Holding she felt she was being drawn to a closer community with people. She had experienced an intense intimacy with nature, often feeling magical, numinous moments of connection and breakthrough out of the blue. And then, with the deep bond with her granddaughter providing a kind of bridge to a larger human community, Leah found that she was drawn to individuals and groups of people who were out in nature and physically active. She joined a group of hikers who took long hikes every Saturday in the beautiful northern California area in which she lived. She joined several walking tours in Europe with family and friends. Leah also became interested in local environmental issues, and worked with groups of people who were active in these areas. Note that Leah had not *decided* that she should be more physical, or that she should become environmentally active; rather, she was drawn towards these new involvements and relationships out of the deeper connection and sense of belonging that she had experienced in the Spreading.

The experience of being beckoned into a new depth in your self and the world, which begins with the Unsettling, continues with the Holding, but now we are drawn toward the fuller living expression of our deeper union with the world. It is up to each of us to pay attention to how the new inner compass of the Holding speaks to us, shows us and draws us towards robust fulfillment of the new possibilities that have opened to us. Nurturing a state of being that is keenly attentive to signs of promise-filled directions, even as we remain relaxed and open, can strengthen our attunement to when and where we are beckoned.

Another development we may experience in the Holding is the growth in our capacity for empathy, for feeling the truth, pain, joy and needs of others. Closely related to the phenomenon of contact-at-a-distance, described in the Spreading, the Holding shows us how it is that we can now feel, to a greater degree than in our previous world, the experience of other people, the life of a flower or animal, the presence of a mountain, etc., as though from within our self. We become aware of other ways of receiving information, such as intuition and direct knowing.

Being affirmed and received as our true self, which we experience in the Holding, strengthens our trust in our self and in life in general. Again, we can feel more open and flexible, less in need of controlling outcomes according to certain preconceptions that we hold about the way things should happen.

It may be that our lives change in visible ways with the Holding. We may find ourselves in new jobs, or moving to another location; maybe we take up new interests and activities, or we begin to expand our relationships. It's also possible that our lives don't change in any outer, concrete ways with the Holding, but we nevertheless experience our lives quite differently. We may find that our values have shifted, and even though we continue with the same job, activities and relationships, we start spending more time with our families or we make sure we have more time with close friends or with a certain activity that we find personally fulfilling. We may feel more playful and buoyant, delighting in the deeper sense of interconnection and intimacy with the world. Our senses may feel intensified and a simple walk may bring us greater pleasure than we can remember.

There are a couple of important things to keep in mind when you find your life changing in these ways. One has to do with the phenomenon of being pulled or drawn towards new situations or ways of being. This kind of change is not brought about because you've rejected your former life. Rather, it more that you find you have outgrown that way of being and a new way is calling you. In the midst of such changes other people in your life may not understand what you're going through. They may feel threatened by your changes or personally rejected.

You may recall in Dawn's story how she found herself wanting more than the "craft fair scene" was offering her. She wanted something deeper in her art and her personal relationships. She began spending more time in her studio instead of spending so much time with her fabric art friends and attending the craft fairs. She was clear that this was not a rejection of these friends. She was pulled to something different and she honored that pull by how she spent her time. Similarly, Dawn gradually discovered that she was being drawn towards a more urban area to live. It's possible that friends and acquaintances from her many years in a small rural town could feel threatened, confused or even rejected by Dawn's move. Understanding the nature of these reactions can help you stay loyal to the beckoning pull that is drawing you into a deeper relationship with your self and the world.

Resettling

In the Holding, we experience a kind of "resettling." It is important to recognize the difference between this resettling and the attempts to feel better that we often make in the Unsettling. In the Holding we are not trying to regain equilibrium as we might have done in the Unsettling. We are not trying to fill an emptiness or lack that we are feeling. In the Unsettling we are attempting to resettle on our *own* terms, without having to first enter the unknown, or to be, for quite a period of time, in a state of 'not-knowing.' By contrast, in the Holding we are being drawn towards something new and unknown, rather than trying to change how we feel or moderate our sense of discomfort.

In the Holding we step into our deeper self and begin to relate in a new way with the world around us. We live in this new relationship, exercising our new talents and capacities, until perhaps we outgrow this way of being as well. At this point, the cycle of Deep Change begins all over again.

Leah's experience of Deep Change occurred several years ago. Recently, over tea, reflecting on that time in her life and where she is now, she told me the following:

> *You know, it doesn't end there. Eighty percent of my life is within the abundance and fullness that I arrived into some years ago. And in twenty percent of my life, I am again seeking, searching for what I know not. But because of my first journey, I now have more faith to trust my longing and know that it is a gift and I need to follow it without knowing the outcome—but knowing it will lead me to greater fulfillment of some kind.*

It is possible for us to move through multiple cycles of Deep Change in our lives, though usually in varying degrees of intensity. Each time we move through the complete cycle of Deep Change, our new self-and-world relationship that comes into being is of a larger breadth and depth than the preceding one. This successive increase in amplitude shows how we expand and grow. Each time we grow beyond our present self-and-world, and through the seven major shifts we transcend ourselves and enter a new relationship with the world.

It is also possible for people to live their entire lives and never experience Deep Change. There are several wonderful people in my life who do not recognize having had this experience. The larger dimensions that beckon us in Deep Change are primarily mysterious to us, and we cannot know another person's destiny or the deeper workings of their life. It's just good to know that there may be some people in your life that will not relate to your experiences of Deep Change, and may even be threatened by it or aspects of it.

As we experience the Holding, it is wise, I think, to remember our earlier images of life *going down the drain,* of feeling that our lives were being emptied of meaning, connection and purpose. Recognize that those currents and waves, those same forces that were pulling you down into the *hole in your ocean,* were not only serving on behalf of your longing but *originated* from the larger dimension that is now holding you in its supportive and appreciative embrace.

Deep Change demands our participation in a sacred and powerful movement of transformation, wherein we surrender who we thought we were, who we wanted to be, and who we thought we should be. We have to embrace a willingness to be nothing, and then, wonder of wonders, we arrive in a new land, feeling refreshed and wanted and deeply connected! We find ourselves in a more real connection with our world and with a more secure sense of belonging.

The time may come when you outgrow your new self-and-world structure. Hopefully, as you are beckoned into yet another new cycle of Deep Change, you will find greater faith and stronger *muscles of allowing awareness* from having come to know the journey we've explored here. Just as you have many depths and dimensions within you, so too does our world have dimensions that need us and are calling us to bring our unique awareness into their waiting potential. Each new dimension of the world that we spread into is characterized by relatively greater and greater possible interconnections, and when our essential individual spark of awareness lights up those interconnections, we co-create new things, ideas, ways of being, and new kinds of worlds.

> *Our life is an apprenticeship to the truth that around every circle another can be drawn; that there is no end in nature, but every end is a beginning; that there is always another dawn risen on mid-noon, and under every deep a lower deep opens.*
>
> *—Ralph Waldo Emerson*

Conclusion

Deep change is transformative. This means that we are changed in an intrinsic way. We are not reshuffling or rearranging the design of our life. We are not just adding new skills or things to our life. We are changing the *way* we are experiencing our self and our world. We discover the opening to this new way of being from within a new depth that becomes available to us when we let go of our known self-and-world. Leaving our familiar world before we know where we are going is the profound challenge of Deep Change.

With Deep Change we *transcend* ourselves; we go beyond ourselves and expand. There is a common belief that transcending involves *rising above* ourselves. However, through the seven shifts of Deep Change, we find that our expansion occurs from a new *depth* in ourselves, meaning that we first go down before we expand (spread) out into a larger breadth of being. This understanding is very important because when you feel a longing to grow and become more fully connected to the world, it can be very confusing to experience the pull *down* into *the hole in your ocean.* This downward pull feels like the wrong direction, but now, as we grasp the whole cycle of Deep Change, we can see and hopefully trust that *in and down is where we first need to go.*

You Are Not a Solo Act

Here's an essential dynamic of Deep Change that we need to fully digest: The currents drawing us through the seven shifts *originate* from that deeper dimension in the world with which we long to enter and join. This means that in Deep Change, we are not a solo act. The very force we yearn to connect with is coaxing us to join with it, and we now know that this force is *other than* our individual self and larger than it.

Other kinds of change are often characterized by the fact that we are using our own imaginative and creative powers to draw what we desire to us. And these kinds of situations may or may not involve a transforming or transcending kind of change. They may or may not require surrendering to a larger force, emblematic of Deep Change.

This difference is important to understand because in our Western culture we are far more comfortable with experiences in which we feel empowered as our own agents of change and "in control." We feel greater anxiety when we are experiencing change that is not under our control. In Deep Change we are ultimately asked to surrender to the drawing power of an Otherness, that is, a force greater and more powerful than our singular self. And at the time of our deepest surrender, we don't know what we are letting go into. It often feels like we will fall into oblivion or nothingness, but then discover, in the falling, that we are held within and belong to an expanded dimension of the world. Understanding the nature and necessity of this surrender in Deep Change helps us to appreciate its challenges and—importantly—to have the faith required to stay the course safely.

In our collective belief that we should be the masters of our own destiny, we often misunderstand people who are in the throes of Deep Change. (And, conversely, you may have felt misunderstood by those around you in your journey of Deep Change.) As friends or loved ones, we want them to pull out of it, get a grip, think positively. Suggestions such as these come out of our concern and love for those we see suffering, but if someone is being called to Deep Change, he or she needs something entirely different from us. It is usually our own fears of the unknown that make it hard for us to be present, attentive to and supportive of others' Deep Change cycles. If we can acknowledge that a friend in Deep Change is being drawn by and into a larger and more powerful dimension, and that something transformative and sacred is occurring, we can perhaps be more present with him or her in a fruitful way, in a way that is on the side of the forces of growth and transformation.

Understanding the whole movement of Deep Change, we also see that our surrender into a larger otherness is not a collapse, nor do we disappear or become absorbed. Rather, our surrender turns out to be a willingness to join with a greater breadth, to participate as an essential and wanted partner in a dance of co-creation. As we let go of what has separated us from the world, we spread into a larger dimension and are gifted with new possibilities, with connection and belonging while the larger otherness is gifted with our unique spark of awareness.

Individuation

Deep Change beckons us into a new phase of individuation. Through the seven shifts, we have forged the capacity to open to the possibility of being nothing, leaning into this possibility with wide-awake awareness. And in this deeper letting go of who we thought we were or should be we discover a more essential self, one that now has the capacity to spread into and join with a new dimension of the world. This whole process takes tremendous courage and disciplined muscles of awareness. Free of our familiar identity and ways of coping, we are more naked and willing to be vulnerable. We are more able to be open to the unknown, curious and alert, but not controlling, as we are drawn into new territories and possibilities that we could not have imagined before our arrival. This new kind of maturity is what allows us to expand into the beckoning breadth of the larger otherness, freely uniting with it while at the same time knowing, with greater clarity and certainty, that we are real and greatly desired.

True Self and Authentic Community

One of the many unexpected gifts of our new maturity is the experience of realizing more of our essential self while simultaneously feeling a heightened sense of authentic community. We all long to feel valued for being our true self while, at the same time, having a real membership in a meaningful world. And we often feel that these two–essential self and community–are opposite poles of some kind and that they need to be balanced by making tradeoffs between one or both of them. In marriages, for example, couples sense that they need to "give up" some sense of their individual identity in the service of maintaining their union. While certain kinds of compromise are clearly necessary when we are living with others, the cycle of Deep Change shows us what at first seems like a paradox–that as we become more of our essential self we open into a greater sense of authentic community.

Authentic community means the sense of community that we have not thought up, have not exerted personal effort to create; rather, this kind of community consciousness naturally comes from our capacity to spontaneously spread into deeper dimensions of the world. Recall that in the cycle of Deep Change, what enables our fulfillment of fresh freedom and deeper belonging is our capacity to spread into the *unknown next moment.* And what supports our ability to spread is our willingness to open to the next moment, freed of our familiar ways of perceiving our self and our world. In other words, we do not project forward through our habitual meanings, stories and ideas about how and why things are as they are. We could say that we encounter the next moment "naively," or "projection-free."

There is an important teaching here, one that can guide us in practicing the dynamics of the Releasing and the Spreading, even when we are not in the throes of Deep Change, so that we may consciously develop what I am calling "no projection zones." No projection zones are states of being in which we can feel and express our own truth as well as experiencing the truth of another person(s), free of our own imposed meanings and judgments about our experience and that of the other person.

This is very important to understand, because there is great confusion around what it means to be "true to our self," what it means to "express our feelings," and what it means to "be responsible for our feelings." For example, let's look at a time in which you were aware that you felt angry. In *dwelling* with your anger in a mode free of projections, you would not be repressing your experience of it. You would not be judging yourself for feeling anger, and you would not be blaming anyone else for it. Nor would you be "acting out" in attempts to feel relief from it or to try to get someone else to relieve you of it. You would not make conclusions or analyses about why you were feeling this anger. Rather, you would let yourself describe what you're feeling, be curious about it, respecting that it carries some kind of truth about your experience even while you are assuming that you do not necessarily know the whole of that truth.

It is the habitual meanings and judgments that we attribute to our felt experiences and to other people that impede our ability to genuinely connect with ourselves and the world. Released from the constraints of our habitual stories and meanings, our feelings freely move into and with the next unknown moment in ways we cannot pre-determine. Space opens around us that is free of our projections, into which the truth of our individual experience can spread and expand. And in this clear space, empty of our meanings and judgments, we not only are being true to our own experience but we can feel the experience of the other person on his or her terms. We are no longer experiencing that person through the veil of our projections.

You've probably had these moments where suddenly you may feel as though you are truly seeing the other person for the first time. Here we are describing how these moments happen. A new possibility for real connection occurs, and in this moment of meeting, we are each definitely separate individuals with our own truths, *and* we are intimately experiencing the truth of the other.

Many books and workshops are available today, on how to communicate in ways that mirror what I am describing here. The dynamics of Deep Change affirm for us that the gifts of developing the capabilities to be with our self and others in this way, can fulfill our longing to be true to our self, while being received as who we are and simultaneously experiencing authentic connection with others in our lives.

The Call of Deeper Dimensions

There are multitudinous dimensions to the world that most of us are not normally aware of. Yet with each experience of Deep Change we become available to at least catch a glimpse of these other, deeper dimensions. At these times we can experience a feeling of being refreshed and renewed, or as some have described it, "a window has suddenly been washed clean." The world appears as new, while at the same time it is the same as before. Some people report experiencing their familiar world as if with a greater intensity of light, pervading everything, so that everything they perceive is now "shimmering" or "sparkling." Could it be that when the our familiar identity drops away, we experience the world more intensely, with greater freshness and brightness than before?

The cycle of Deep Change reveals that although we usually cannot see or feel the deeper dimensions in the world, they are always present, beckoning us to join with them. Many of us are being called into Deep Change, and it is time that we recognize when and how in our everyday lives this call is showing up. It's not just appearing within specific spiritual practices, in monastic settings, nor only in extraordinary circumstances. The call of the deeper dimensions in the world is felt right in the midst of our everyday lives. It is just that we often miss the signs and thus, miss the way in. Many are being called, and also, many people are being thwarted in this call due to the lack of knowledge, understanding and support.

We have many ways of covering over the threshold experiences of Deep Change, one of which is the great proliferation of pharmaceuticals in our culture, which constitutes a serious matter that demands our attention, education and action. Through indiscriminant and uneducated prescription of these drugs, many of us are being robbed of the fulfillment of our deepest longings for greater meaning, connection and belonging. These drugs may dull our immediate pain and discontent—or make us indifferent to being discontent, but in the long run this dulling blocks our entry into our true future.

Many of us have given up. The pain of our past has covered over our openings to new depths to such an extent that we cannot feel our longings for deeper connection and belonging. But the spark of longing still resides within those of us who are caged in our own despair and doubt, and we can still be available to the pull of other dimensions beckoning us into deeper fulfillment. If these words resonate with you, please know that you have not been abandoned. The fact that you are reading this book reveals that your longing, no matter how faint, is alive and is exerting its pull upon you.

We all long for the numinous, for a greater connection to life, to feel more alive and meaningfully engaged with our world. We long for those moments in our everyday life that surprise us, delight us, take our breath away, humble us, as something truly new breaks through into our normal experience. We long to move into that space where the world sparkles and we know without a doubt that something very real has touched us and that we belong unquestionably to it. Deep Change is calling us into the experiences we most deeply long for.

Deep Change of the Collective

Deep Change is not only a natural dynamic of growth and transformation for individuals but also for groups of people: families, organizations, businesses, whole communities, countries and cultures. In other words, deeper dimensions in the world call us not only as individuals but collectively as well. This is an enormous topic, but one that needs to be introduced here.

Many economists, social philosophers, environmentalists and political scientists are observing that our culture is deteriorating and may well be facing collapse. The incidence of depression and anxiety has risen to epidemic proportions. The most commonly heard explanation is that it is caused by our fast-paced lifestyle. There is tremendous pressure to succeed, growing economic, health and environmental concerns, and a breakdown of support systems such as family and community. While all of these are contributing factors I would argue that our entire culture is poised on the brink of Deep Change. We are, as a people, Unsettled. Crises everywhere are pointing to the fact that we are not who we thought we were or want to be.

The tragedy of 911 sent shock waves of a new kind which have reverberated across the country, touching everyone's life. Old symbols of our country's strength and invulnerability have been destroyed, making us realize we are not invincible. Furthermore, as a nation our first response to this attack on our own soil has been very similar to how we often, as individuals, initially respond to a crisis that heralds Deep Change. We have circled our wagons, pointing blame, reasserting our military strength to cover over the sense of helplessness we have experienced. We want nothing more than to return to the self-and-world-structure we lived and which flourished almost since we established our independence.

Many people feel the flaws, the lacks and the cracks in our American way of life. We feel we are coming up empty in relation to the myriad problems our country faces. A Deep Change has taken hold of our nation. We are no longer able to cover over our new sense of lack. America in the throes of Deep Change is being pulled into the currents of its hole in the ocean. Our response to this Unsettling has largely amounted to rearranging the deck chairs on the Titanic. It's terrifying for us to accept that we may be sinking as a nation but our usual ways of proceeding only perpetuate the status quo, and we miss the way in to a possible new relationship with the world.

Understanding the whole cycle of Deep Change can offer us a way to have faith in the Unsettling and Unraveling we observe and feel around us. If we dare to look closely and to listen deeply, perhaps we'll discover a greater yearning. Perhaps as a people we can recognize and articulate America's collective longing for a new possibility, a longing to be more meaningfully connected to the world. And if we dare pursue it, maybe we'll discover together, a new relationship with the world and ourselves. Could it be that a larger dimension is already longing for America to come into a new depth? All of this could be very good news but only if we, as a people, learn to cooperate with the dynamics of Deep Change.

It is critical that we begin to look at our collective lives through the lens of Deep Change. How can we as a people lean into the unknown dimensions that are beckoning us into a new future with the world? How can we recognize and embrace these efforts on behalf of opening and accepting that we are helpless to carry on as usual? And how can we recognize and not be tempted to support the efforts on behalf of resignation, which we now know are only disguised efforts to stay in control and keep things the same.

We are coming up empty in so many ways, and yet we keep rearranging the chairs on our national deck, trying not to look into the unknown that is opening all around us. Can we, the people, look collectively at what appears to be the bottom of an empty treasure chest, and have the faith that this is but a false bottom, and that true riches are hidden beneath it?

With all our technological advances and power we really know very little about how to envision an unknown future, together. However, understanding the shifts of Deep Change and their interrelationships can point us towards ways to listen; this understanding can show us what we need to watch for, the importance of feeling our insecurity, uncertainty, emptiness and grief without drawing conclusions about what they mean. We need, as a people, to let go of our past ways of being, leaning into unknown futures without self-destructing along the way. We, as a people, may then discover a more essential national identity and destiny, one that would spread and join with the world. This would be a new phase of maturation for America.

The central question is how do we nurture the opening to new depths that are calling for America to come into a truer essence, one with a greater capacity to unite with and to cooperate and collaborate with those deeper dimensions that are longing to support new ways to live together fruitfully, sustainably and compassionately on this planet?

It's important to recognize the existence of real efforts already working on behalf of the kind of envisioning required to support Deep Change on a cultural and even global scale. There are individuals and groups seriously exploring ways we can collectively listen to what is longing to come into presence and how, together, we can envision the longing of America that is wanting to draw us into a new relationship with ourselves and the world. There are individuals and groups creating new kinds of technologies designed to guide us in how to listen and think and envision collectively. They are truly the new pioneers; some of these individuals and organizations are identified in the Resources Guide in this book.

In our Western tradition, there is a great emphasis on the primacy of individual freedoms. If as a people we were to collectively turn towards the currents of Deep Change, and learn to trust and cooperate with these forces, we would come into a new kind of freedom—the freedom to assemble, to willingly join with others in ways that create new worlds, worlds of greater possibilities, deeper connections, expanded creativity and unquestioned membership for all.

The above discussion barely touches on the broader applications of the cycle of Deep Change. My wish is that it will stimulate questions and conversations and further research. There are many other applications, parallels and implications of the cycle of Deep Change, some of which may have been stirred in you.

In revealing our natural yet miraculous human capacity to join with deeper dimensions in the world, this book is a beginning. My hope is that others will join me in continuing to explore the nature and varieties of the experience of Deep Change and how we can share and use this knowledge to bring us all into a deeper humanity, with our true heritage of compassion, connection and belonging.

Appendix:

Diagrams of the Movement of Deep Change

Introduction to Diagrams

As you look over the diagrams in the following pages, keep in mind that they are showing the movements of a person's awareness as they journey through Deep Change. Also keep in mind that because the material in this book is describing what we experience as we cooperate with the forces of Deep Change, the diagrams are also descriptive, not prescriptive, nor are they theoretical constructs.

Ideally, you would be looking at a video of the diagrams, which would reveal more clearly the movement and relationships among the shifts. If they do not lend further clarity for you or further support an understanding of your experience, feel free to pass them by. They are included here in the appendix because some people have found them helpful.

Remember that this two-dimensional representation of the movements of Deep Change do not depict the multi-dimensionality of the experience.

Diagram A: Familiar Self-and-World (p.188)

This sphere represents our known self-and-world structure when we are **not** in the throes of Deep Change. The outer border of the sphere represents the boundary between the unknown and our known self-and-world. Here, our sense of our self-and-world is basically stable, intact. We could say that our desire to stay on familiar ground and our desire to change are equal, and so the *status quo* holds. We go along in our lives with a relative sense that things are okay.

Diagram B: Shifts 1, 2, 3 and 4 (p.189)

This figure represents our familiar self-and-world, but as compromised. There is now a disequilibrium, wherein the forces of change are stronger than the forces to stay the same. What had felt intact is now compromised, and we first feel Unsettled.

Shift 1: This illustrates being out in a place or in a depth beyond our familiar self-and-world, indicating the arrival of a free-floating longing. This longing creates a real possibility for greater connection and belonging for us, but it resides as a possibility in a dimension deeper than that of our familiar self-and-world. Therefore, while we feel its presence, we cannot access its fulfillment from within our familiar world. This gives rise simultaneously to what is initially experienced as a flaw or felt lack in our familiar world, which is indicated by the hole in the sphere (2).

Shift 2: The Opening. Here we discover that as we allow our experience of the Unsettling, and accept our felt lack, our sense of a flaw or emptiness now becomes an opening into unknown depths within our self. Since the lack is *felt*, to accept it means feeling it on its own terms, which involves a movement into our own felt experience.

Shift 3: The Unraveling. Once we allow ourselves to dwell within the opening to unknown personal depths of Shift 2, we become available to a pull down into these depths of personal subjective experience. In this descent, the tapestry of our self-identity loosens and begins to fall away. The diagram represents this descent as a movement through unknown, undetermined space within our known self-and-world structure, often experienced as some kind of vertical cavity.

Shift 4: The Stilling. We come to the end of our familiar self-and-world with nothing else in sight. We stand at this threshold looking out into what appears to be nothing. Here we are suspended at the threshold, or demarcation, between two different worlds and ways of being, but we have not fully yet let go into the unknown. It feels as though there is nothing before us, no horizon, just a vast vacuous space.

Diagram C: Shifts 5, 6 and 7 (p.190)

In a more realistic depiction of the experience of Deep Change, this diagram would not show the former known self-and-world because those have unraveled. But to illustrate the relationships between Shifts 1-4 and 5-7, it is necessary to keep this image as if it were within the new self-and-world structure. This comparison of the old and new structures also serves to illustrate the relative increase in breadth and amplitude that is included in the new structure. In short, the comparison shows how we grow, how we transcend ourselves in Deep Change.

Shift 5: The Releasing. We experience a release into "fresh freedom." This is a point of radical discontinuity when we open to the *unknown next moment* in a mode of being that is free of our familiar structure, and we experience continuing on, beyond the ending of our known identity, yet as a very real individuality.

Shift 6: The Spreading. We find that our fresh freedom has the wondrous capacity to spread throughout the deeper dimension that we are released into. As our unique spark of awareness shoots out into a world, flush with radical relatedness, we join intimately with this world even while we maintain our individuality.

Shift 7: The Holding. We experience being *received, wanted and held* by a larger otherness that has beckoned us into its depths. In the joining of our individual spark with the larger dimension, a new self-and-world structure comes into being, and our free-floating longing (Shift 1) for deeper connection and belonging is fulfilled. Notice the contrast in the expanse of breadth now included in our new structure with that of our former familiar structure.

Diagram D: Two Revolutions of Deep Change (p.191)

Notice that with each revolution, the breadth, the amplitude included in our self-and-world structure expands. This is how we grow and transcend ourselves. With each cycle of Deep Change, we spread throughout deeper dimensions that are characterized by successively greater possibilities for interconnections and relatedness, and therefore our expansion brings us an increased capacity for intimate contact, fuller meaning and deeper belonging.

Diagram A.
Familiar Self and World

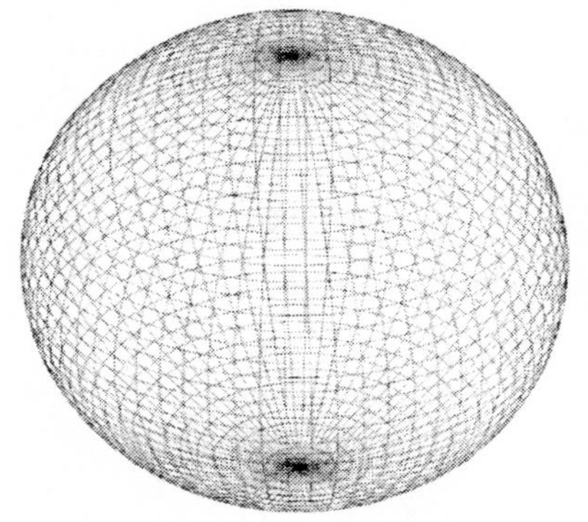

Diagram B.
Shifts 1, 2, 3 and 4

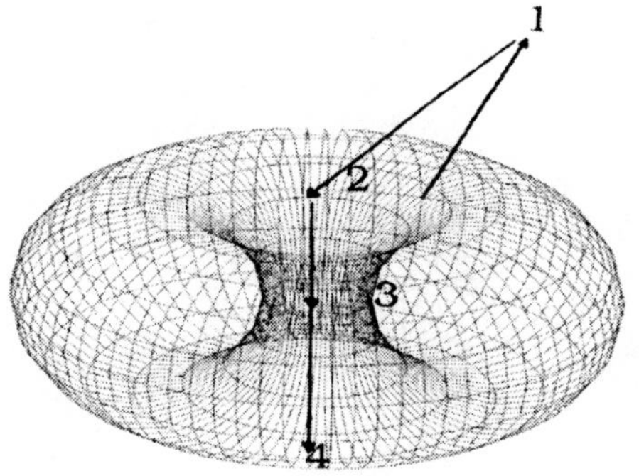

Diagram C.
Shifts 5, 6 and 7

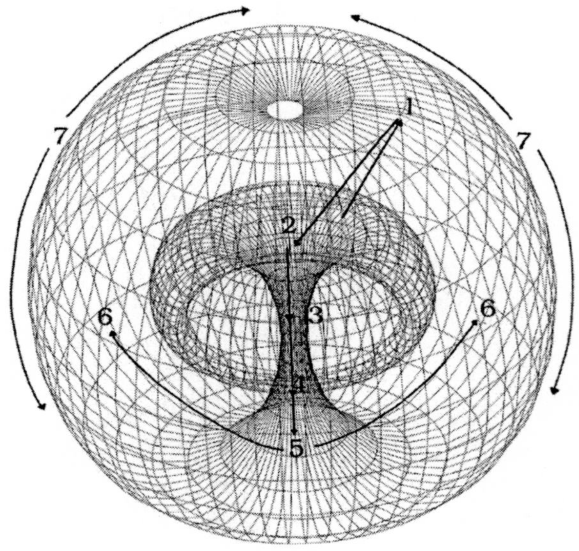

Diagram D.
Two Revolutions of Deep Change

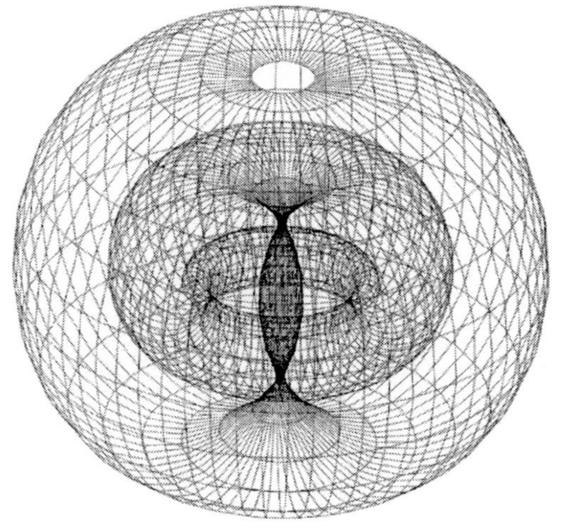

Partial Resource List

The following includes works that I have found supportive of the process of Deep Change. It is by no means comprehensive.

Bailey, J.K.: *Already on Holy Ground,* 1996, Hazelden Information & Educational Services

Bolen, Jean Shinoda: *The Millionth Circle*, 1999, Conari Press

Chodron, Pema: *When Things Fall Apart*, and *The Places That Scare You,* Shambhala.

Daumal, Rene: *Mount Analogue*, 1952, City Lights Books

Dillard, Annie: *Holy the Firm* and *Teaching a Stone to Talk,* 1982, Perennial Library.

Gendlin, Eugine: *Focusing*, 1978, Bantam Books

Harper, Ralph: *On Presence*, 1991, Trinity Press International

Johnson, Robert: *Balancing Heaven and Earth,* 1998, HarperSanFrancisco.

Kierkegaard, Soren, *The Concept of Anxiety*, trans. Thone, R. and Anderson, A, 1980, Private University Press

Kuhlewind, George: *From Normal to Healthy*, 1983, Lindisfarne Press

Novak, Michael: *The Experience of Nothingness*, 1970, Harper Colophon Book.

O'Donohue, John: *Eternal Echoes,* 1999, Cliff Street Books.

Palmer, Parker: *A Hidden Wholeness*, 2004, Jossey-Bass.

Paz, Octavio: *In Search of the Present,* 1990, Nobel Lecture, Harcourt Bruce and Company.

Rilke, Rainer, Marie: *Letters to a Young Poet,*

Roberts, Bernadette*: The Experience of No-Self;* 1983, SUNY Press

Sardello, Robert: *Facing the World with Soul,* 1995, HarperCollins

Simmons, Philip: *Learning to Fall,* 2002, Bantam Books

Watts, Andrew: *The Wisdom of Insecurity,* 1951, Pantheon Books

The poetry, prose and essays of the following:

Wendell Berry

William Blake

Paulo Coelho

Ralph Waldo Emerson

Pablo Neruda

John O'Donohue

Mary Oliver

Rainer Maria Rilke

Rumi and other Sufi mystics

David Wagoner

Walt Whitman

David Whyte

Embodied Imagination Dream Work by Robert Bosnak.

The Rosen Bodywork Method.

Acknowledgments

First, I wish to thank my wonderful family: my mother, Darlene, sisters Peggy and Polly, and my brother Courtney for his weekly phone calls during my own periods of Deep Change. All of them, including their spouses and offspring, have given me a lifetime of support, faith and love. I have deep appreciation for my editor, Hal Zina Bennett, for his patience, artful skills and belief in this project. Immense gratitude to Amedeo Giorigi for creating such a profound methodology for investigating human experience, one that is rigorous and faithful to what it means to be a human being, and special thanks for chairing my dissertation committee, without which this material would never have become visible. Great thanks to Kevin Kelly for the diagrams, and to Adam Freeman for the "donut." I have deep gratitude for my psychotherapy clients over the many years of my practice, for their trust, courage and authenticity. Special thanks to the Wednesday night group. Warmest gratitude to two special friends for their time and honest sharing; you know who you are. And thank you to the subjects in my original research, who will remain anonymous. A heartfelt embrace to Kristy and Kevin and Anne and Steve for their many years of unconditional love and support. Robust thanks to Bonnie for the many nourishing meals and love. Warmest hugs full of thanks to my many friends in Mendocino County who have showered me with loving encouragement. And I extend a thankful acknowledgement to Larry Harris for supporting my first steps towards the creation of this project. Inevitably there will be those who have lent me their generous support but who I'll discover I've regrettably neglected to mention. I apologize ahead of time for my forgetfulness. Finally, I wish to thank my new Santa Barbara community for holding me in such a warm embrace. Many thanks to Mary Ellen Kelly and Caryl Casbon for being such wise and heartfelt cheerleaders at the finish line.

About the Author

Susan P. Plummer, PhD, has been a psychotherapist in private practice for the past 25 years in northern California, as well as the director of a hospice agency. She has a life-long interest in transformation, both for individuals and communities. She presently lives in Santa Barbara, California where she is the director of the Alliance for Living and Dying Well.

Susan is available for presentations, lectures and workshops. She can be reached at:

Plummer.DeepChange.Susan@gmail.com